GALLUP
MAJOR TRENDS & EVENTS
The Pulse of Our Nation: 1900 to the Present

Immigration

GALLUP
MAJOR TRENDS & EVENTS
The Pulse of Our Nation: 1900 to the Present

Abortion

Drug & Alcohol Abuse

Health Care

Immigration

Marriage & Family Issues

Obesity

Race Relations

Technology

GALLUP
MAJOR TRENDS & EVENTS
The Pulse of Our Nation: 1900 to the Present

Immigration

Roger E. Hernandez

Produced by OTTN Publishing, Stockton, New Jersey

Mason Crest Publishers
370 Reed Road
Broomall, PA 19008
www.masoncrest.com

First printing

1 3 5 7 9 8 6 4 2

Library of Congress Cataloging-in-Publication Data

Hernández, Roger E.
  Immigration / Roger E. Hernandez.
      p. cm. — (Gallup major trends and events)
  Includes bibliographical references and index.
  ISBN-13: 978-1-59084-965-1 (hard cover)
  ISBN-10: 1-59084-965-5 (hard cover)
  1. United States—Emigration and immigration—Juvenile literature. 2.
Immigrants—United States—Juvenile literature. I. Title. II. Series.
  JV6455.H43 2005
  305.8'00973—dc22
                        2005016300

TABLE OF CONTENTS

Introduction

By Alec Gallup, Chairman, The Gallup Poll

In ways both obvious and subtle, the United States of today differs significantly from the United States that existed at the turn of the 20th century. In 1900, for example, America had not yet taken its place among the world's most influential nations; today the United States stands by itself as the globe's lone superpower. The 1900 census counted about 76 million Americans, largely drawn from white European peoples such as the English, Irish, and Germans; 100 years later the U.S. population was approaching 300 million, and one in every eight residents was of Hispanic origin. In the first years of the 20th century, American society offered women few opportunities to pursue professional careers, and, in fact, women had not yet gained the right to vote. Though slavery had been abolished, black Americans 100 years ago continued to be treated as second-class citizens, particularly in the South, where the Jim Crow laws that would endure for another half-century kept the races separate and unequal.

The physical texture and the pace of American life, too, were much different 100 years ago—or, for that matter, even 50 years ago. Accelerating technological and scientific progress, a hallmark of modern times, has made possible a host of innovations that Americans today take for granted but that would have been unimaginable three generations ago—from brain scans to microwave ovens to cell phones, laptop computers, and the Internet.

No less important than the material, social, and political changes the United States has witnessed over the past century are the changes in American attitudes and perceptions. For example, the way Americans relate to their government and their fellow citizens, how they view marriage and child-rearing norms, where they set the boundary between society's responsibilities and the individual's rights and freedoms—all are key components of Americans' evolving understanding of their nation and its place in the world.

The books in this series examine important issues that have perennially concerned (and sometimes confounded) Americans since the turn of the 20th century. Each volume draws on an array of sources to provide vivid detail and historical context. But, as suggested by the series title, GALLUP MAJOR TRENDS AND EVENTS: THE PULSE OF OUR NATION, 1900 TO THE PRESENT, these books make particular use of the Gallup Organization's vast archive of polling data.

There is perhaps no better source for tracking and understanding American public opinion than Gallup, a name that has been synonymous with opinion polling for seven decades. Over the years, Gallup has elicited responses from more than 3.5 million people on more than 125,000 questions. In 1936 the organization, then known as the American Institute of Public Opinion, emerged into the spotlight when it correctly predicted that Franklin Roosevelt would be reelected president of the United States. This directly contradicted the well-respected Literary Digest Poll, which had announced that Alfred Landon, governor of Kansas, would not only become president but would win in a landslide. Since then Gallup polls have not simply been a fixture in election polling and analysis; they have also cast light on public opinion regarding a broad variety of social, economic, and cultural issues.

Polling results tend to be most noticed during political campaigns or in the wake of important events; during these times, polling provides snapshots of public opinion. This series, however, is more concerned with long-term attitude trends than with the responses to breaking news. Thus data from many years of Gallup polls are used to trace the evolution of American attitudes. How, for example, have Americans historically viewed immigration? Did attitudes toward foreign newcomers shift during the Great Depression, after the 1941 Japanese attack on Pearl Harbor, or after the terrorist attacks of September 11, 2001? Do opinions on immigration vary across different age, gender, and ethnic groups?

Or, taking another particularly divisive issue treated in this series, what did Americans think about abortion during the many decades the procedure was generally illegal? How has public opinion changed since the Supreme Court's landmark 1973 *Roe v. Wade* decision? How many Americans now favor overturning *Roe*?

By understanding where we as a society have been, we can better understand where we are—and, sometimes, where we are going.

1

A COUNTRY OF NEWCOMERS

A man wakes up at dawn, opens his front door and, after looking back to his still sleeping wife and four children in their tiny apartment, heads out in the early morning light. Someone, drunk perhaps, is passed out on the street. A gang of hoodlums stands menacingly on a corner.

Yet life in this inner-city neighborhood encompasses more than just crime and substance abuse. As the man walks down the block, shopkeepers born in the same country as he begin to open their stores, which sell the food he grew up eating. The sights, sounds, and smells remind him of his faraway homeland. He smiles inside.

The man is an immigrant going to his American job, to do backbreaking work that pays barely enough to keep a roof over his family and food on their table. But he has a dream, one impossible to realize in the troubled nation he left behind.

He dreams that his children will be free of the hardships he has endured, and that they will get the education he never had. And he dreams

(Opposite) With their meager belongings in tow, an immigrant family gazes across the water toward New York from a dock on Ellis Island, circa 1912. For more than 200 years the dream of a better life in America has been a powerful pull for people from all over the world.

they will grow up to live over there, in the big homes on the fancy side of town where the Americans live lives of plenty.

For that dream, he works.

The man could have been an Irish immigrant named O'Hara, living in New York City's notorious Five Points district in 1852 and working to lay railroad tracks that made mass transportation possible from coast to coast.

Or maybe he was Olaf, arrived from Sweden in 1882 and living briefly in Chicago before heading off to the

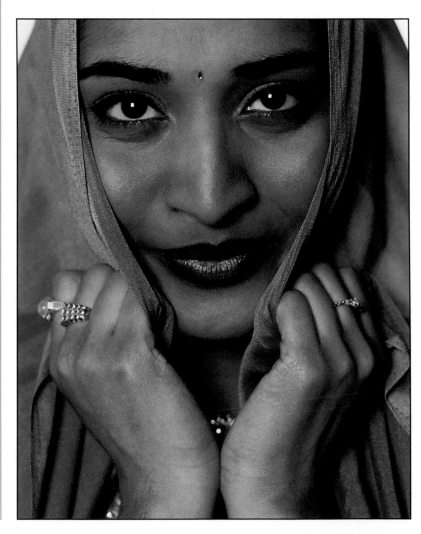

Among legal immigrants to the United States, India was the second-leading country of birth (behind Mexico) in the first years of the 21st century. According to the Office of Immigration Statistics, more than 190,000 Indian immigrants were admitted into the United States between 2001 and 2003.

rich farmlands of Minnesota to raise wheat and help turn the Midwest into the breadbasket of America.

He could have been named Giuseppe and been an Italian immigrant living in the teeming Lower East Side of Manhattan in 1912, with a job in one of the garment factories that powered the country's industrial economy.

Or he could be living today, a Mexican immigrant named José living in East Los Angeles, working to pick lettuce that will end up washed clean and wrapped in plastic at supermarkets everywhere. Many consumers would not give a thought to the immigrants who made such a luxury possible.

The story of folks coming to the United States from foreign countries to seek a better life is a recurring one in American history. Newcomers have always helped shape the country's identity — in fact, the United States was founded by men whose British ancestors arrived just a few generations before the Declaration of Independence was signed in 1776. Their accomplishments form one of the oldest and most basic elements of the American character.

However, since the revolutionary era there have been contributions by other peoples that have shaped the national identity. During the civil rights movement of the 1950s and 1960s, black Americans fought for the rights the Founding Fathers promised two centuries earlier. These Americans, whose African forebears were brought across the Atlantic Ocean as slaves, championed a struggle for racial equality that is part of the American legacy, too.

Immigration is also part of that legacy. Upon the foundation laid down by men of British ancestry in 1776 and made to reach its promise by many Americans since, immigrants from all over the world have helped build the United States of today.

As much as anything else, the United States is a nation of immigrants, of freedom-seekers escaping political or religious oppression, of poor families looking for economic opportunities that do not exist in "the old country," of brilliant scientists or gifted artists who believe that in the United States they are freer to use their talent than in any other place on earth.

Immigrants like Albert Einstein (originally from Austria), renowned architect I. M. Pei (China), acclaimed author Frank McCourt (Ireland), and the legendary Coca-Cola executive Roberto Goizueta (Cuba) all made significant achievements while living in the United States. Others helped shape American popular culture, from the Norwegian-born Knute Rockne, who became part of football legend as a University of Notre Dame coach, to the Oscar-nominated Indian American film director M. Night Shyamalan, to Sergey Brin, the Russian co-founder of Internet search engine Google. Even the vast majority of immigrants who never became famous made lasting contributions. They carried out the hard work in factories, construction sites, and farm fields that made their new country rich and strong. And they contributed to the vibrant mix of cultures, ethnic backgrounds, and traditions that make up the fabric of the United States today. What would the American diet be without frankfurters, pizza, and burritos?

THREE ERAS OF IMMIGRATION

Immigration in U.S. history can be divided into three waves. The first began in the 1830s, slowed during the Civil War (1861–65), and started up again after the war. The vast majority of immigrants in those years came from the nations of northwestern Europe. First to arrive en masse were Irish Catholics, 2 million of whom had arrived by the time the Civil War started. By that time they were being slightly outnumbered by Germans seeking economic opportunities or escaping the political turmoil of their homeland. After the war the Germans and Irish kept coming but were joined by another people from northwestern Europe, the Scandinavians. Smaller numbers of Asians, Latin

Americans, and eastern and southern Europeans also arrived during this wave.

The late 1890s marked a major shift in immigration. By that decade people from eastern and southern Europe—Italy, Russia, Poland, and the Austro-Hungarian Empire—started to outnumber those from northern and western Europe. It was the start of a second wave of immigrants. A staggering 12 million of them arrived between 1900 and World War I, proportionally the largest influx of immigrants in U.S. history.

The upheaval caused by World War I (1914–18) and the restrictive immigration laws that followed during the 1920s ended the second immigration wave. For most of the 1930s and 1940s, the number of new arrivals sank to the lowest levels since the 1820s, before the first immigrant wave arrived and helped turn the United States into a nation of immigrants. During the next two decades the numbers started crawling back up, especially after the Immigration and Nationality Act of 1965 increased the number of foreigners permitted to immigrate. These increases mark the beginning of the third wave.

This recent wave has continued into the present day. Most immigrants today are from Latin America and Asia. Others come from eastern Europe or Africa. Some 20 million people have arrived since 1970, contributing to a total of 60 million people who have immigrated to the United States since the 1830s. In a manner similar to how they responded to previous immigrant waves, many Americans in recent years have not approved of the high numbers of newcomers.

Gallup polls have shown that since the mid-1980s, most Americans either want immigration decreased or kept at current levels. In 1995, during an era of strong anti-immigrant sentiment, the number of people who wanted it decreased peaked at 65 percent. Just less than a quarter of respondents (24 percent) said immigration should remain at the current level, while only 7 percent thought it should increase. Gallup recorded a much

Opinions on Immigration

"In your view, should immigration be kept at its present level, increased or decreased?"

1995

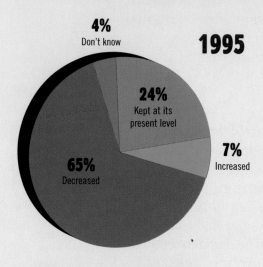

4%
Don't know

24%
Kept at its present level

7%
Increased

65%
Decreased

Poll taken June 1995; 1,006 total respondents
Source: The Gallup Organization

2000

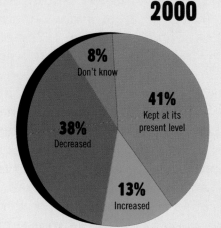

8%
Don't know

41%
Kept at its present level

38%
Decreased

13%
Increased

Poll taken September 2000; 1,007 total respondents
Source: The Gallup Organization

2005

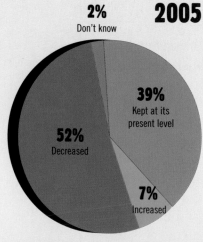

2%
Don't know

39%
Kept at its present level

52%
Decreased

7%
Increased

Note: This question had slightly different wording than the two polls above.

Poll taken January 2005; 1,005 total respondents
Source: The Gallup Organization

better mood regarding immigration five years later, when 41 percent of respondents said they wanted it kept at current levels and 13 percent wanted it to increase. By January 2005, with slightly different wording in the question, opinion charted midway between the extremes of 1995 and 2000: 52 percent wanted immigration cut, 39 percent wanted it to stay the same, and 7 percent wanted to allow more immigrants.

IMMIGRATION ANXIETIES

Why are so many Americans today upset over the number of immigrants? "[T]he surge in immigration (particularly the illegal variety) during the last 20 years has likely played a role in many Americans becoming dissatisfied with the current level of immigration," explained Darren K. Carlson, government and politics editor for the Gallup Organization. The nearly 30 million foreign-born persons living in the United States today—a group that includes naturalized citizens, permanent residents (green card holders), and an estimated 11 million illegal immigrants—are a source of concern for economic and social reasons.

Nativists argue that the newcomers are stealing jobs from native-born Americans and that they are too different from ordinary citizens to assimilate. Organizations favoring an end to immigration have published numerous studies that say immigrants willing to work at low wages are taking jobs from Americans, and that they are staying to themselves in their own neighborhoods, refusing to assimilate, and only speaking their own languages. But there are pro-immigration advocates on the other side of the debate, and the studies they cite reach the exact opposite conclusions—that hard-working immigrants contribute to the U.S. economy, that they are assimilating as rapidly as previous generations of immigrants did, and that the only linguistic problem they face is that their English-speaking children will forget their ancestral tongue entirely.

Nearly every ethnic or national group that has come to the United States in large numbers has initially faced discrimination. Over the years, however, some European groups with a long history of immigration have fully assimilated. In the 1830s and 1840s, for example, job-seeking Irish immigrants were greeted with signs saying "No Irish need apply"; today more than 1 in 10 Americans is of Irish ancestry, according to the 2000 census. And these descendants of a once-ostracized group are universally regarded as fully American. Will the same thing happen with the Asian and Latin American immigrants of the new millennium? Will, for example, the descendants of brown-skinned mestizos from Guatemala become a part of the American mainstream?

There are plenty of similarities between present-day immigrants and the immigrants who preceded them. Like the Irish and Italians of past generations, the Hispanics and Asians of today came to seek a better life, face accusations that they refuse to assimilate, often live in neighborhoods that reinforce their ethnic identity, and have children who in one way or another are more "Americanized" than they.

But there are also major differences between the new immigrant experience and the old. Today's immigrants can watch television or listen to radio in their native languages, which makes it easier for them to maintain ties to their culture and language. There are also new multicultural values that encourage immigrants to hold on to their ethnic roots.

Where is this wave of immigrants headed? As the years pass, will they or their children become "real" Americans? How much of their ethnic identity should immigrants keep? Figuring out the answers to these questions often entails discussing the American "melting pot," a famous metaphor for how immigrants and their children assimilate. The descendants of immigrants from previous generations are said to have become part of this melting pot because they "blended in" with the rest of the population. But blending in didn't happen easily during the first years after the immigrants' forefathers arrived, neither for the Irish in the middle of the 19th century nor for the Italians and Jews during the first few decades of the 20th. They lived according to their traditions apart from mainstream Americans, many of whom believed these newcomers would never assimilate.

Even today some members of those "old" ethnic groups maintain their traditions through the food they eat and the family ties they keep with their ancestral nations. Is the real story of U.S. immigration that it resembles not a melting pot but a salad bowl, in which different ingredients mix together yet maintain their distinctive flavor? The question may never be answered, but one thing is certain: throughout its history the United States has embraced its immigrants as much as it has been ambivalent about them.

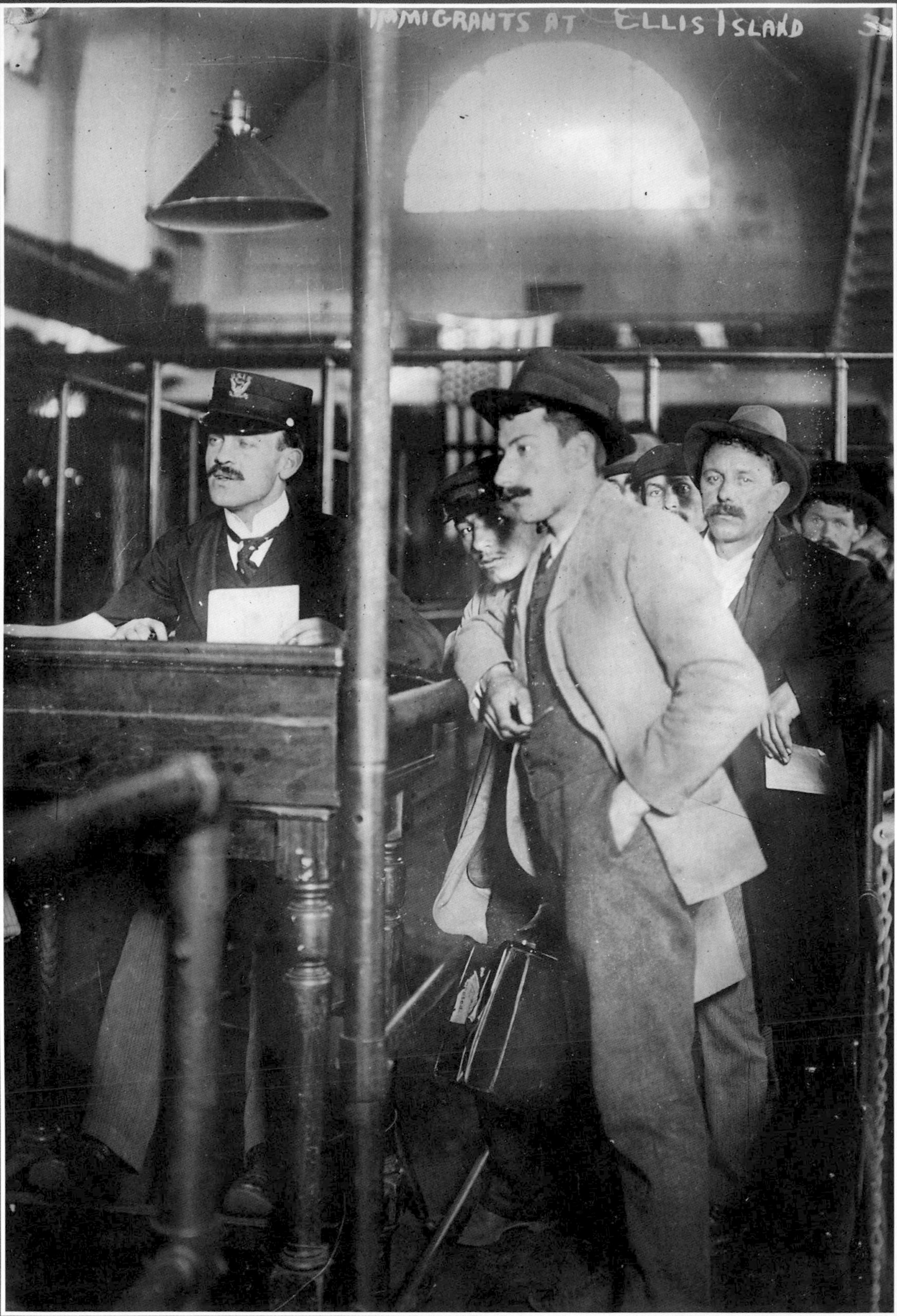
IMMIGRANTS AT ELLIS ISLAND

2

ELLIS ISLAND'S GATE

A total of 857,046 foreigners arrived in the United States in 1903, setting a new immigration record. Ellis Island, an immigration station in New York Bay, held the distinction of processing many of these newcomers that year. It remained the primary immigration center during subsequent years, when between 1905 and 1914 the annual total of immigrants to the United States broke the one million mark six times. Nearly 40 percent of U.S. citizens have at least one ancestor who passed through the doors of Ellis Island.

Along with the Statue of Liberty, Ellis Island remains the most potent symbol of American immigration. The immigration center first opened in 1892, but the original wooden buildings burned down five years later. A new station constructed of brick opened on December 17, 1900. Nearly 2,500 immigrants passed through that first day. The number soon tripled. More buildings were added as the number of new arrivals increased and new immigration laws made processing them more complicated.

(Opposite) Hopeful immigrants wait in line to be processed, Ellis Island. To gain admission into the United States, immigrants had to undergo a medical exam and answer questions designed to screen out those with a criminal past as well as those likely to become public charges. Beginning in 1903, anarchists were also supposed to be sent home.

Everyone who came through Ellis Island underwent inspections that determined whether they would be allowed to remain in the United States. Immediately upon arrival, they had to stand in long lines to undergo a medical exam, in accordance with the Immigration Act of 1891, which banned anyone with a contagious disease. Those who passed were then questioned about their past, because the same law also prohibited entry by convicted criminals and anyone likely to become a public charge. A year later, another law barred people deemed to be mentally unstable, and beginning in 1903, yet another law screened immigrants for their political beliefs. A passage of this law excluded "anarchists, or persons who believe in, or advocate, the overthrow by force or violence the government of the United States, or of all government. . . ."

During Ellis Island's peak years, about one-fifth of immigrants were sent up what were called the Stairs of Separation into its Great Hall for further questioning. Here people from across the globe requested officials in dozens of different languages to allow them into the United States. Others suspected of having contagious diseases were sent to the hospital on the premises. Most immigrants were eventually sent back down to a joyful reunion with family members who were already admitted. But 2 percent never made it down the stairs. They were refused admission and put on a ship to go back home, while the other 98 percent looked forward to the beginning of a new life.

Between 1900 and the start of World War I in 1914, a total of 12 million people passed through Ellis Island and other processing centers throughout the United States. Some 203,000 of the newcomers in 1903 were northwestern Europeans—Scandinavians, Germans, Irish, and English—who had been arriving on the East Coast for three-quarters of a century. However, an even greater proportion of immigrants during that year were eastern and southern Europeans—Italians, Jews, Poles, and other peoples. The huge number of these newcomers and the fact that they hailed from a different region of Europe made them a distinct wave in U.S. immigration.

JOURNEYS FROM ITALY

Italian newcomers were one of the prominent groups of the new immigration wave. There were few Italian immigrants before the 1890s (they were mostly artisans and shopkeepers from relatively prosperous northern Italy), but after Ellis Island opened, the trickle became a flood. Approximately 4 million Italians arrived between the time the doors opened and the early 1920s. The majority were landless peasants from the poor and mostly rural south of Italy and the equally impoverished, rural island of Sicily.

For the most part, however, the Italians did not seek farm work in the United States, but rather the jobs that were available near the port where they arrived. For most immigrants that port was in New York City. More than a third of Italian immigrants stayed in neighborhoods in the metropolitan area—in Brooklyn or the Bronx, across the Hudson River in New Jersey, and especially in Lower Manhattan.

The best known of those neighborhoods is Manhattan's Little Italy, whose streets were filled with Italian shopkeepers and street vendors. A distinguishing feature of Italian life in New York was the village association. People from the same village tended to live in the same neighborhood, sometimes even in the same tenement building. This living arrangement preserved ancient village traditions as well as relationships among families who had known each other back home in Italy.

One ancient tradition preserved by immigrants was the Catholic *festa*, which celebrated a village's patron saint with a yearly feast. On *festa* days, neighborhood residents—many who were once fellow villagers—

Mulberry Street, in the heart of Manhattan's Little Italy section, circa 1900. More than a third of the approximately 4 million Italians who immigrated to the United States between the 1890s and the early 1920s remained in the New York City metropolitan area.

would stage a procession with thousands of people following the image of the saint through city streets. "Around the corner came a band of musicians with green cock-feathers in hats set rakishly over fierce, sunburnt faces," wrote journalist Jacob Riis in an 1899 account of the festival of San Donato on Mulberry Street, the heart of Little Italy. "A raft of boys walked in front, abreast of two bored policemen, stepping in time to the music. Four men carried a silk-fringed banner with evident pride." This tradition survives today, with Little Italy's San Gennaro Festival attracting thousands every year.

For many Italian immigrants, being outdoors on their village saint's day was a chance to get away from the gloom of their tenement rooms. Their workplaces were usually just as gloomy. Because they had been farmers, they did not bring the skills needed in the industrial economy of urban America, so they took jobs as laborers. According to a Library of Congress online overview of immigration, 90 percent of the laborers employed by New York's Department of Public Works in 1890 were Italian immigrants. Other laborers, most of whom were women, worked in unsafe and low-paying sweatshops. When the infamous Triangle Shirtwaist Factory fire killed 146 immigrants in New York in 1911, about half of the victims were young Italian women. Many Italians who did not work in sweatshops or for the city were self-employed. The fruit vendor pushing his cart through the street became an oft-stereotyped figure of Italian American life.

The Italian fruit vendor was one of the more harmless stereotypes, however. Italian immigrants also had to contend with racial theories claiming that dark-haired immigrants from "backwards" countries in the Mediterranean were genetically inferior to people of northern European heritage.

Yet Italians, like the Irish and German immigrants who preceded them, became part of the American fabric as the decades wore on. By the 1940s there was a new generation of U.S.-born Italian Americans, and many of them served in World War II. From that decade on, says a report from the Library of Congress, "the children of Italian immigrants could be found in all regions of the U.S., in almost every career and nearly every walk of life." Luminaries such as New York Yankees great Joe DiMaggio, singer Frank Sinatra, composer Henry Mancini, and heavyweight boxing champion Rocky Marciano rank among the best-known figures of American culture.

While Italians were by far the most numerous immigrants from the Mediterranean, they were joined by immigrants from Greece and Turkey. More than 350,000 Greeks and over 290,000 Turks arrived between 1900 and 1920. Like other immigrants, Greeks typically started out as low-paid laborers or factory workers. Yet before long, many of them had acquired restaurants throughout the northeastern states. The region is still dotted with diners and restaurants owned by Greek immigrants.

JEWISH ORIGINS

Another people that arrived in large numbers during this period were Jewish immigrants, who hailed from different countries—primarily Poland, Russia, and Romania—but were united by a common religion and culture. The exact number of Jewish immigrants is hard to pin down because newcomers were only required to give U.S. authorities their country of origin, not their religion. A report by the Library of Congress estimates that 3 million Jews from eastern Europe arrived between 1880 and 1924.

Few Jewish immigrants returned to their homelands. In fact, they had the lowest rate of return of any major immigrant group, and for good reason. The Jews had been marginalized and oppressed in Russia and the rest of eastern Europe for years, and anti-Semitism often erupted in tragic violence. During pogroms in Russia and neighboring countries, attackers wiped out entire Jewish villages and killed thousands in urban ghettos. Jews who fled the pogroms and made it to the United States came to stay for good.

An established Jewish community, mostly made up of German Jews, was already in place when the eastern European Jews began arriving in large numbers. But members of that established community, who had already accumulated some wealth, were a generation or more removed from their immigrant past and struggled to relate to the poverty-stricken and uneducated newcomers. Eager to establish roots in their new country, eastern European Jews set about creating their own world, much of it based on the source of the community's identity—its religion. How individuals practiced religion varied, however. Some immigrants were Orthodox Jews, who lived in strict accordance with religious mandates (including kosher dietary laws) and were easily distinguishable by their black clothing and the long beards worn by the men. Other Jewish immigrants were more secular and more selective in observing certain traditions.

The majority of Jewish immigrants to the United States remained in New York City. By 1920 about half of all American Jews lived there, making up one-quarter of all New Yorkers.

Like the Irish and Italians, Jews formed their largest ethnic enclave in Lower Manhattan. In 1910 the neighborhood known as the Lower East Side was home to

A Jewish immigrant family assembles garters in their tenement home in Manhattan's Lower East Side.

more than 500,000 Jews squeezed into 1.5 square miles. There they lived in five- and six-story walk-up tenements lacking hot water, often with a single shared bathroom on each floor.

It was a thoroughly Jewish neighborhood, not unlike other urban ethnic enclaves where immigrants congregated to socialize, shop, and worship with people like themselves. But the economic opportunities of the Lower East Side were different from those of Little Italy or those of the Irish neighborhoods half a century earlier. Jewish immigrants were prevented from entering major professions by anti-Semitic "gentlemen's agreements." They responded by employing an entrepreneurial strategy that created their own opportunities. In the Lower East Side, Jewish businessmen soon became owners not only of grocery stores and other neighborhood shops, but also of banks, factories, and even the tenements in which they lived. It has been estimated that three-quarters of New York's approximately 300,000 garment workers before World War I were Jewish, as were the owners of most of the 16,000 factories.

A combination of business success and a desire for education helped Jewish immigrants and their U.S.-born children move up in American society. Some joined the ranks of the most prominent figures of their time. Scientist Jonas Salk (developer of the polio vaccine), Supreme Court justice Felix Frankfurter, novelist Isaac Bashevis Singer, composer Irving Berlin (whose most famous song is "God Bless America"), and Hollywood studio heads Samuel Goldwyn, Louis B. Mayer, and the four brothers who

Vienna-born Felix Frankfurter immigrated to the United States with his Austrian Jewish family in 1894. Frankfurter served as an associate justice of the U.S. Supreme Court from 1939 to 1962.

founded Warner Brothers Studios all left a profound imprint on American culture.

COMING FROM THE EAST

In addition to the Jewish population, there were two dozen nationalities among the immigrants from eastern Europe. The most numerous were the Poles, but there were also Russians, Ukrainians, and the diverse peoples that made up the Austro-Hungarian Empire (1867–1918)—German-speaking Austrians; Magyar-speaking Hungarians; Romanians (who spoke a language heavily influenced by Latin); and Slavic groups such as Czechs, Croats, Serbs, Bulgars, and others. Perhaps about 3 million of them immigrated to the United States during the Ellis Island years.

Figuring out the immigration totals of these groups is difficult because the authorities lumped together most of the ethnicities of Austria-Hungary under the single category "Other central Europe." Likewise, it is difficult to determine the number of Polish immigrants between 1900 and 1918, a period during which Poland was not an independent nation. Instead of being labeled Polish immigrants, newcomers were labeled according to their occupying country at that time, which could have been Germany, Russia, or Austria-Hungary. The division of the Polish homeland was a catalyst for the exodus of many Poles during the Ellis Island years, along with political persecution, land shortages, and high unemployment.

Polish immigrants had much in common with the Irish immigrants who arrived a half-century before them: they were generally poor and ruled by others, yet proud of their national identity, committed to fighting for their home country's independence, and set on preserving their Catholic faith. Some Poles kept their agricultural vocations after they arrived, going to work on farms on the East Coast and in the Midwest. The majority, however, found work in the mills, slaughterhouses,

Some Polish immigrants, like this woman shucking corn in Fairfield County, Connecticut, sought to re-create the farming life they had known in the old country. More, however, gravitated toward the industrial cities of the Northeast and Midwest, where they found jobs in factories, mills, and slaughterhouses.

and factories of the Industrial Belt, a U.S. region extending across the north of the country from the East Coast to the cities of the Midwest.

Cities around the Great Lakes attracted many Polish immigrants. Buffalo had approximately 70,000 Polish immigrants by 1905, most of them residents of an eastside neighborhood known as Polonia, which had one of the highest concentrations of Poles in the United States. Other Great Lakes cities recording large Polish populations that year were Chicago (250,000), Milwaukee (65,000), and Detroit (50,000). Outside the Great Lakes area, New York City recorded 150,000 Polish-born residents, while Pittsburgh was home to 70,000.

At first, a large number of Polish immigrants were more preoccupied with liberating their homeland than with assimilating to U.S. society. But after they helped reestablish an independent Poland following the end of World War I, many turned their attention to American affairs. Members of a new U.S.-born generation preferred to see themselves as Polish Americans rather than as Poles.

ARRIVING ON THE WEST COAST

Leading up to World War I, there was a separate influx of immigrants crossing the Pacific Ocean from Asia. These newcomers settled primarily on the West Coast, whose main port of entry, San Francisco, served as a counterpart to New York City. The 1880 and 1890 censuses show that the city was home to 20 percent of the country's Chinese immigrants, who were second only to the Japanese as the largest Asian immigrant group living in the United States. San Francisco was also the first U.S. city to have a Chinatown, founded in the 1850s.

Like other immigrant groups, the Chinese encountered prejudice and even violent attacks. Growing resentment against this group led to a series of laws restricting Chinese immigration. The most prohibitive were the Naturalization Act of 1870, which restricted the Chinese from obtaining U.S. citizenship, and the Chinese Exclusion Act of 1882, which aimed to end immigration from China.

Although they were greater in number than the Chinese immigrants, Japanese immigrants were slower to settle in San Francisco or other West Coast cities during the late 19th and early 20th centuries. Rather than heading directly to the mainland, the majority of Japanese migrated to Hawaii, a U.S. territory that had not yet become a state. As more immigrants arrived, the Japanese eventually replaced native Hawaiians as the most numerous group on the island chain.

Anti-Chinese sentiment ran high at the time this cartoon—which depicts a Chinese man attempting to sneak into the United States in various disguises—was created. In 1910, five years after the cartoon appeared in the humor magazine *Puck*, the Angel Island Immigration Station opened in San Francisco Bay. Officials there turned away the vast majority of would-be immigrants from China.

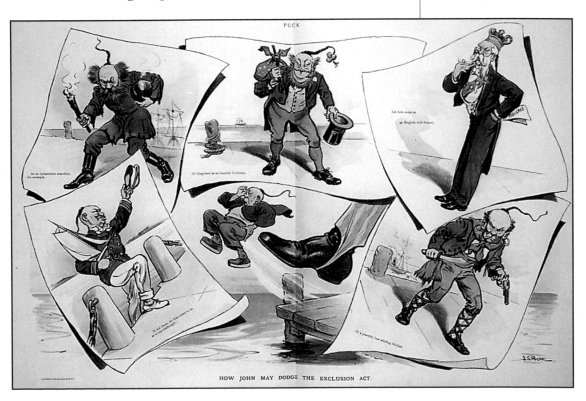

HOW JOHN MAY DODGE THE EXCLUSION ACT.

In time the Japanese settled in greater numbers along the Pacific coast. Between 1900 and 1925 more than 100,000 Japanese immigrated to the United States. Like the Chinese, however, they faced animosity from nativists, along with a series of immigration restrictions. A "gentlemen's agreement" made in 1908 effectively ended immigration from Japan, with the exception of Japanese who had relatives already living in the United States.

In spite of the immigration restrictions, many Asians still journeyed across the vast Pacific Ocean hoping to find a new home in the United States. The Chinese Exclusion Act, in particular, had loopholes that certain classes of Chinese (including teachers, merchants, and the wealthy elite) tried to exploit. In part to cope with the unwanted increase in Asian immigration, authorities set up the Angel Island Immigration Station in San Francisco Bay in 1910. The station achieved its designed purpose: the overwhelming majority of the 1.75 million Chinese immigrants processed between 1910 and 1940 were denied entry.

THE GATES CONTINUE TO CLOSE

During this period, immigrants from other parts of the world experienced a similar backlash. Nativists were upset over the growing numbers of immigrants. In 1910 foreign-born people made up 15 percent of the total U.S. population (compared with just 10 percent in 2000). Ten years later, the 1920 census found that 13.9 million U.S. residents had been born overseas; many others, while born in the United States, had two foreign-born parents (15.7 million) or one foreign-born parent (7 million). Thus immigrants or residents with at least one immigrant parent totaled 36.6 million—about a third of the entire U.S. population.

To some degree, foreigners had grown used to the backlash. Ever since the arrival of Irish Catholics in the 1830s, immigrants had been blamed for crime, for taking jobs away from Americans, for bringing diseases, even for having the wrong religion. But by the first decades of the 20th century, the country's xenophobes had another, more urgent concern: they feared that immigrants were also planning a radical takeover of the U.S. government.

These were indeed troubled times. In 1919 immigrants were blamed when postal officials intercepted 38 bombs that had been mailed to American politicians and business leaders. A few weeks later an explosive blew up outside the house of Attorney General A. Mitchell Palmer. The following year two Italian immigrants and known anarchists named Nicola Sacco and Bartolomeo Vanzetti were arrested for the murders of a paymaster and guard at a shoe factory in South Braintree, Massachusetts. (Both men were convicted in a 1921 trial whose fairness is still hotly debated today.) In response to this apparent insurgent threat, the attorney general ordered the arrest of thousands of subversives—many of them immigrants—in what became known as the Palmer Raids during 1919 and 1920. Some foreigners were deported, but most were eventually released.

Fear of immigrants remained. Congressman Albert Johnson of Washington worried that because the country was letting in newcomers from countries that did not embrace or even know democracy, "our capacity to maintain our cherished institutions [stood] diluted by a stream of alien blood." Johnson became the chief promoter of two bills—one in 1921 and the other in 1924—that were

Nicola Sacco (right) and Bartolomeo Vanzetti, photographed in 1926, the year before their executions for a robbery and double murder in South Braintree, Massachusetts. Many historians believe the two Italian immigrants—both avowed anarchists—were innocent, but their arrest and trial fueled fears of radical immigrants.

THE ELLIS ISLAND OF THE WEST COAST

The Chinese Exclusion Act of 1882 was the culmination of a movement to end Chinese immigration to the United States. However, the act had a number of loopholes. For example, it barred entry only to Chinese designated as laborers. Those in certain professions, such as teachers, could still immigrate under the terms of the act, provided they obtained from the Chinese government a certificate attesting to their eligible status. Well-connected Chinese could obtain such certificates; forgeries were also a concern. The Angel Island Immigration Station, the West Coast's lesser-known counterpart to Ellis Island, was established largely to handle thousands of Chinese seeking entry, in addition to the Japanese, Russians, Indians, Koreans, Australians, and Filipinos also arriving on the West Coast.

As a result of the passage of the Chinese Exclusion Act, the Chinese received the worst treatment at Angel Island. Immigration inspectors, who anticipated that Chinese newcomers would try to circumvent the act by posing as members of exempt professions, refined a system of interrogation much more grueling than that faced by other immigrants.

"Over the course of several hours or even days, the applicant would be asked about minute details only a genuine applicant would know about—their family history, location of the village, their homes," explains the Angel Island Immigration Foundation. "[W]itnesses—other family members living in the United States—would be called forward to corroborate these answers. Any deviation from the testimony would prolong questioning or throw the entire case into doubt and put the applicant at risk of deportation, and possibly everyone else in the family connected to the applicant as well." Until all questions were satisfactorily answered, Chinese immigrants were held as prisoners for weeks or months in cramped, unsanitary barracks worse than any holding cell at Ellis Island.

passed to cut back immigration. The laws set up a new quota system that favored immigrants from northwestern Europe at the expense of Italians, Jews, Poles, Asians, and other groups not from the region.

In the wake of this legislation, the number of Italian entrants dropped from more than 222,000 in 1920 to 40,000 in 1922 and only 5,520 in 1925. Immigration from other restricted countries, such as Japan and China, dropped just as dramatically. But even among the favored countries, immigration fell below the levels seen in previous decades. Only half a million immigrants were admitted into the United States during the 1930s, compared with the 4 million who had come during the 1920s.

In effect, an open door policy spanning 100 years had come to an end. Between 1901 and 1930, the United States had welcomed more than 18.6 million people, but for the next generation, it would largely close its doors.

3

NEW NEWCOMERS

The 1930s and 1940s were tough decades for immigrants. The number of people who arrived on U.S. shores in search of the American dream decreased not only because of the stricter laws but also because of the economic devastation wrought by the Great Depression (lasting from 1929 to the early 1940s) and the upheaval of World War II (1939–45).

In 1933, at the depth of the Great Depression, one in four Americans was unemployed, and the lack of jobs discouraged people from immigrating to the United States. That same year the United States admitted only 23,068 entrants, the lowest single-year total since 1831. The number rose slightly in the late 1930s as the economy gradually revived, but then the turmoil of World War II cut it back down. Only 23,725 immigrants arrived in 1943, and fewer than 5,000 were from Europe. With the continent torn by war and German submarines prowling the Atlantic, Europeans had a difficult time even imagining their escape.

Because Japan was a U.S. enemy during the war, immigration from that country dipped to

(Opposite) As smoke billows from the battleship *West Virginia*, hit by more than half a dozen Japanese torpedoes and bombs, a small craft pulls a sailor from the waters of Pearl Harbor, December 7, 1941. The surprise Japanese attack pushed the United States into World War II. Among the consequences for immigration were the repeal of the Chinese Exclusion Act and the creation of a program to attract Mexican agricultural laborers to the United States.

35

just a few dozen people between 1942 and 1946. Before that period more than 400,000 Japanese immigrants had entered the United States or its possessions, many settling in Hawaii. Japanese immigration had come to a virtual standstill with the quota laws of the 1920s. By the 1930s more than half of the Japanese in the United States were *Nisei*, the Japanese label for American-born children of Japanese immigrants. At home, they lived in a Japanese world with their parents, but they were also a part of the broader American culture.

Their peaceful lives were shattered after the Japanese attacked Pearl Harbor on December 7, 1941, bringing the United States into World War II. Thousands of Japanese Americans were arrested in the days that followed. Then, beginning in 1942, more than 125,000 individuals—Japanese-born as well as U.S.-born citizens—were forced to move to internment camps.

"This large-scale imprisonment of U.S. citizens solely on the basis of their ancestry was met with almost universal approval by the non–Japanese American population," says a Library of Congress analysis. Life in the camps was difficult. "[I]nternees slept in barracks or small compartments with no running water, took their meals in vast mess halls, and went about most of their daily business in public," the same report explains. The camps had their own houses of worship, schools, businesses, and newspapers, but all of these were surrounded by barbed wire and armed guards. Ironically, at the same time that the Japanese American detainees were being victimized, the all-Nisei 442nd Regimental Combat Team was fighting in Europe, achieving distinction as one of the most decorated units of its size in the history of the U.S. military.

Meanwhile, treatment improved for immigrants from China, a U.S. ally in the war. President Franklin D. Roosevelt proposed repealing the Chinese Exclusion Act to allow Chinese persons already in the country to

apply for citizenship, but the law in question also set a quota of just 105 Chinese immigrants per year, much lower than the limits imposed on European immigrants. In spite of the low quota, Americans were still wary about the proposal. A 1943 Gallup poll found that just over 41 percent opposed reopening the doors to the Chinese, while just under 41 percent supported it. Nevertheless, in December of that year the law passed, which set the quota but also abolished the Exclusion Act. It was "a landmark in Chinese-American history," wrote Iris Chang in *The Chinese in America: A Narrative History*.

HINTS OF CHANGE

The war years saw an increase in the number of immigrants from Canada and Latin America (although this was easy to overlook given the low overall rate of immigration). Of the 23,725 foreigners who were admitted in 1943, a total of 18,162 came not from Europe, but

Japanese men burn brush at the Manzanar Relocation Center in eastern California. Beginning in 1942, Japanese Americans living on the West Coast were rounded up and sent to internment camps like Manzanar, where they remained in many cases until the end of World War II.

Opinions on Chinese Immigration, 1943

"Should the immigration laws be changed to permit 105 Chinese to enter this country each year and become citizens?"

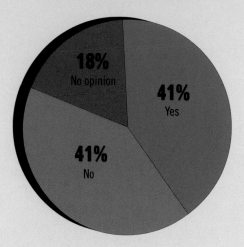

18%
No opinion

41%
Yes

41%
No

Poll taken October 1943; 1,484 total respondents
Source: The Gallup Organization

from the nations of the Western Hemisphere. One reason for this shift was that unlike the Europeans and Asians, whose immigration was restricted by the 1924 law, the people of North, Central, and South America faced no limits. During that period, most of the Western Hemisphere immigrants were from Canada; the next-largest group was from Mexico.

Some 80,000 Mexicans lived in what are now southwestern states after the United States annexed the region following the U.S.-Mexican War (1846–48). These Mexicans were not considered immigrants since they did not migrate to the United States, but rather found themselves on U.S. soil after the end of the war. During most of the 19th century, annual immigration levels from Mexico remained below 1,000, according to official figures. There were probably more entrants not included in these figures, because border inspections were lax. Nonetheless, European immigrants vastly outnumbered Mexican immigrants during the first few years of the 20th century.

However, during the Mexican Revolution of 1910 and the period of instability that followed, the number of Mexicans entering the United States finally began to rise. Between 1910 and 1930, the number of U.S. residents born in Mexico tripled from 200,000 to 600,000, according to the Census Bureau, and there may have been more (the population was hard to count because Mexican immigrants routinely crossed back and forth between the two countries). Whatever the total number, it signaled the first large wave of immigration from Latin America.

One reason Congress imposed no quotas to restrict Mexican immigration was that ranch owners needed cheap labor to harvest the vast farm fields of California and the Southwest. The plan worked during the 1920s. With European and Asian immigration at record lows, Mexican immigration provided a new and much-needed source of low-paid farm labor.

However, when the Great Depression hit, the same laborers who were once valued were now accused of taking desperately needed American jobs. As hostility grew toward Mexican laborers, the government began a repatriation program. "Immigrants were offered free train rides to Mexico, and some went voluntarily, but many were either tricked or coerced into repatriation, and some U.S. citizens were deported simply on suspicion of being Mexican," says a Library of Congress study. "All in all, hundreds of thousands of Mexican immigrants, especially farmworkers, were sent out of the country during the 1930s—many of them the same workers who had been eagerly recruited a decade before."

A decade later, popular opinion shifted and Mexican workers were recruited again. With American

A train car filled with Mexican agricultural workers recruited to help harvest the U.S. sugar beet crop, 1943. Under the bracero program, initially established to help remedy U.S. labor shortages created by World War II, more than 4 million Mexican farm workers came to the United States between 1942 and 1964.

men fighting in World War II and many others—including women—working in U.S. shipyards and munitions factories, farmers again found themselves looking for cheap labor. To remedy that shortage the U.S. and Mexican governments created the bracero program, under which Mexicans could come to the United States as temporary workers. Though paid very low wages, they still earned more than they would have in Mexico. More than 4 million braceros came to work in the United States.

By the 1950s, however, the U.S. government once again reversed its policy toward migrant workers. Under "Operation Wetback" some 4 million Mexicans, as well as Mexican Americans, were deported. Yet

many others stayed—perhaps some 100,000—and still others continued to arrive. By 1956 Mexicans finally outnumbered Canadians as the largest immigrant group from the Western Hemisphere.

Another Spanish-speaking group, Puerto Ricans, started to make their presence felt around this time, too. Puerto Rico had been annexed by the United States after the Spanish-American War of 1898. Beginning in 1917, Puerto Ricans were U.S. citizens by birth, which meant they were no longer considered immigrants. Legally speaking, moving from Puerto Rico to the mainland was the same as moving to New York from New Jersey. However, few Puerto Ricans could afford the fare, and by 1940, there were still fewer than 70,000 Puerto Ricans living in the continental United States.

In subsequent years, cheaper air and sea fares encouraged more Puerto Ricans to leave. By 1950 more than 300,000 Puerto Ricans lived in the United States, and 10 years later the number had nearly tripled. The Puerto Rican community, mostly based in New York, and the Mexican American community, based in the Southwest and California, laid the groundwork for the millions of Hispanics who would arrive decades later.

THE GATE REOPENS

Throughout the 1950s, Americans generally remained wary of immigration, regardless of the tough circumstances facing immigrants. When some 35,000 Hungarians escaped to the United States as political refugees following a failed anti-Soviet uprising in 1956, Americans were lukewarm about letting the Hungarians stay permanently, according to Gallup poll results. Even though Hungarians had taken up arms against the Soviet Union—the U.S. enemy during the Cold War—just over 43 percent of those polled said the refugees should remain subject to deportation laws, while just under 41 percent said laws should be changed to let them stay.

Heritage and Immigration, 1965

How important do you think a person's country of origin should be in determining whether or not someone from another country should be admitted to live in the United States?

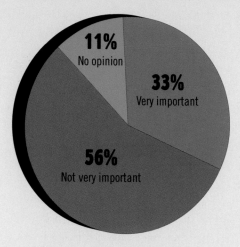

11%
No opinion

33%
Very important

56%
Not very important

Poll taken June 1965; 3,536 total respondents
Source: The Gallup Organization

Under the leadership of President Harry S. Truman, the law was changed, enabling the Hungarians to stay. As early as 1952 Truman had advocated for the right of people to receive asylum in the United States. He also wanted immigration law to show greater favor toward those who had valuable occupational skills or family members already living in the country. These changes, the president hoped, would eliminate the national origins quotas. While the Immigration and Nationality Act of 1952 did not go so far as to eliminate quotas, it did ease quota requirements and made people of all races eligible for naturalization.

The total number of immigrants to the United States averaged about a quarter-million a year during the 1950s, the highest since the restrictive laws of the 1920s.

Meanwhile, the immigrant population continued to shift from being primarily European to Latin American and Asian. More than a fifth of all immigrants in the 1950s were Hispanic, while the proportion of Asians grew from 3 percent of all immigrants in the 1940s to 6 percent in the 1950s.

The anti-immigration mood continued to wane with the election of John F. Kennedy in 1960. As the first president to be a Roman Catholic and a descendant of Irish immigrants, Kennedy supported a more open immigration policy, calling for the abolition of the quota system. After he was assassinated in 1963, his successor, Lyndon B. Johnson, also pushed Congress to end quotas.

A 1965 Gallup poll showed that the public supported Johnson on this issue. A majority of respondents (56 percent) said country of origin was "not very important" when "determining whether or not a person from another country should be admitted to the United States." However, 64 percent of respondents appeared to make an exception to admit people "who escape from Communism." In the early 1960s laws were passed to facilitate the immigration of Cubans escaping Fidel Castro's dictatorship, much like what was done when the Hungarians fled their Communist regime a decade earlier.

With public interest in immigration high, President Johnson signed the Immigration and Nationality Act of 1965, reopening the immigration doors that were shut 40 years earlier. The law replaced national origins quotas with a preference system that granted visas to skilled workers as well as close relatives of U.S. citizens and permanent residents. Quotas on immigration from individual countries were eliminated, but annual caps were set on the total number of immigrants from the New World (120,000) and the Old World (170,000).

After the 1965 law went into effect, the number of people entering the United States went up but did not explode immediately. About 1.8 million immigrants arrived between 1965 and 1969, compared with the total of 1.4 million arriving between 1960 and 1964. Still, the population shift that began in the 1950s was completed by 1970: the number of Asians and Latin Americans arriving that year was more than two times higher than the number of European entrants.

NEW WAVE

Not all Americans welcomed the newcomers during this time. A few months before Congress passed the 1965 law, a Gallup poll showed that 33 percent of Americans wanted immigration decreased. Only 8 percent thought it was a good idea to let more immigrants in, while 39 percent thought the level should stay the same. In a Gallup poll that asked the same question 12 years later, the number of respondents favoring a decrease in immigration rose 9 percentage points.

The results of the Gallup polls certainly were not resounding endorsements of immigration, yet the numbers of immigrants never declined in subsequent years. In fact, immigration soon grew to levels unseen since the early 1900s. Nearly 4.5 million people moved to the United States between 1971 and 1980. European immigration totaled some 800,000 people over that period, much lower than the 1.9 million who came from the Americas and the 1.6 million from Asia. How did Americans respond to this new group of arrivals? With ambivalence, as public opinion indicated in the wake of two major events, the "boat people" crisis and the Mariel Boatlift.

During the "boat people" crisis of 1979, a million people fled the countries of Indochina—Laos, Cambodia, and Vietnam—that had fallen to communism. President Jimmy Carter pledged to double the number of Vietnamese refugees admitted to the United States from 7,000 to 14,000 a month—a plan that drew a mixed reaction from the public. A 1979 Gallup poll

Opinions on Immigration

"In your view, should immigration be kept at its present level, increased or decreased?"

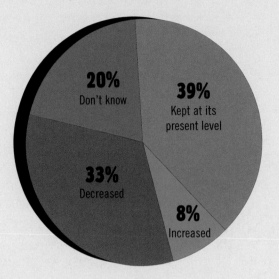

Opinions - 1965

20%
Don't know

39%
Kept at its
present level

33%
Decreased

8%
Increased

Poll taken June 1965; 3,536 total respondents
Source: The Gallup Organization

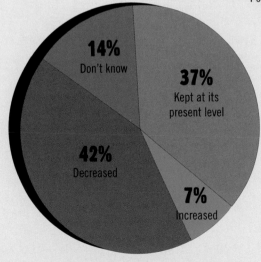

14%
Don't know

37%
Kept at its
present level

42%
Decreased

7%
Increased

Opinions - 1977

Poll taken March 1977; 2,736 total respondents
Source: The Gallup Organization

showed that 57 percent of Americans opposed relaxing immigration policies to let in more "boat people," while only 32 percent favored the measure. On the other hand, 57 percent said their home communities would welcome refugees.

The other major immigration event during this time was the Mariel Boatlift of 1980, when Fidel Castro temporarily lifted restrictions that prohibited Cubans from leaving the island without government permission. More than 125,000 Cubans sailed rickety boats from the port of Mariel, east of Havana, to south Florida. The majority arrived in May and June of that year as the overwhelmed U.S. Coast Guard tried to cope with the swarms of people. It was perhaps the most disorderly episode of mass migration in U.S. history. What made things worse was that Castro had freed some 2,000 hard-core criminals and mixed them in with the rest of the Mariel refugees. Further exacerbating the crisis was the state of the U.S. job market at the time: Americans faced one of the highest jobless rates in decades. When Americans were asked in a Gallup poll if they thought "political refugees should be permitted to immigrate to the U.S. or immigration should be halted until the unemployment rate in the U.S. drops," nearly 66 percent said they wanted immigration halted.

But the immigration numbers continued to rise. Between 1981 and 1990, over 7.3 million immigrants arrived, followed by nearly 9.1 million between 1991 and 2000. That figure set a new record for immigrants in a decade, higher than the 8.8 million who entered between 1901 and 1910.

For some time now, Europeans have constituted a minority of foreign-born U.S. residents, as the gap between immigrants from Europe and elsewhere has continued to widen. Between 1981 and 1990 the number of European entrants dipped to 705,000, while 3.6 million immigrants came from the Western Hemisphere and 2.8 million from Asia. Then, in the

1990s, the downfall of communism in the Soviet Union and eastern Europe left the people of the region free to immigrate; largely as a result, the number of arrivals from Europe shot up to more than 1.3 million. During the same decade, the number of Asian newcomers stayed at roughly 2.8 million, while the number from North, Central, and South America rose to about 4.5 million.

THE CLIMATE TODAY

In the decades since the passage of the Immigration Act of 1965, the law has been fine-tuned several times to change the maximum number of immigrants under the various categories. As of mid-2005, there was no limit on the number of visas available to spouses, unmarried minor children, and parents of U.S. citizens, but there was a cap of 226,000 visas per year for everyone else in the "family preference" category. In addition, 140,000

A fishing boat, its deck packed with Cuban refugees, sails across the Straits of Florida, April 1980. Over the course of six chaotic months, some 125,000 disaffected Cubans left their home-land for south Florida in what became known as the Mariel Boatlift.

Immigration and Unemployment, 1980

Do you feel that political refugees should be permitted to immigrate to the U.S. or that immigration should be halted until the unemployment rate in the U.S. drops?

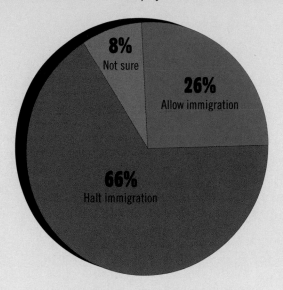

8%
Not sure

26%
Allow immigration

66%
Halt immigration

Poll taken May 1980; 1,582 total respondents
Source: The Gallup Organization

employment-based visas could be given each year, and 70,000 people admitted as refugees. There are also 50,000 "diversity" visas awarded each year to people in countries that send few immigrants to the United States.

One country that clearly does not qualify for the diversity category is Mexico, the largest single source of immigrants to the United States. Between 1993 and 2003 more than 1.6 million Mexicans were recorded to have entered legally. Among Spanish-speaking nations, the Dominican Republic sent the next-highest number over those same years (some 327,500), followed by El Salvador (234,500), Cuba (224,000), and Colombia (148,500). From the non-Hispanic nations of the

Americas, roughly 183,000 Haitian and 174,500 Jamaican newcomers arrived during this period.

In Asia the largest number of immigrants between 1993 and 2003 came from the Philippines (some 530,000), followed by the People's Republic of China, India, and Vietnam. A majority of European immigrants were from formerly Communist nations—especially Russia (174,000) and Poland (160,000). With the exception of Great Britain (168,000), no other European country sent nearly as many immigrants during this period, including traditional sources of immigration like Ireland, Italy, and Germany. African immigrants exceeded 480,000 between 1993 and 2003, a huge increase in migration from previous decades. The three African nations sending the most immigrants were Nigeria, Ethiopia, and Egypt.

By 2000, increases in immigration from various regions of the world lifted the number of foreign-born individuals living in the United States to about 28 million, according to the Census Bureau. A little more than half of this group was from Latin America, while Europeans made up just 15 percent of the foreign-born population (compared with 62 percent in 1970).

How have Americans responded to the increased number of immigrants in recent years? Gallup polls have recorded changing opinions since this new wave of immigration began. In 1986, a year when Americans were beginning to take note of the soaring immigration numbers, a survey found that a bit less than half the public (49 percent) wanted fewer immigrants, while only 7 percent wanted immigration to increase.

As the number of newcomers continued to rise, so did anti-immigrant sentiment. It was particularly strong in California, where many people worried that the exploding immigrant population was becoming a drain on the economy and a threat to the culture. Voters demanded action, particularly against the undocumented, or illegal, immigrants, and politicians rode the crest of the anti-immigrant wave. It all came to a head in 1994 when the state's voters approved Proposition 187, which denied most public services—such as enrollment in public schools and non-emergency health care—to illegal immigrants and their children. The measure was nearly enacted in 1995, but a federal court ruled it unconstitutional because it exceeded the state's jurisdiction regarding immigration law. Although Proposition 187 was only a state initiative, it sparked debate across the country.

During this time, the U.S. Congress seemed to be listening to the Proposition 187 supporters as the House

Applauding a 1999 court decision striking down key provisions of California's Proposition 187 are, from left, Ernesto Zedillo, the president of Mexico; Antonio Villaraigosa, speaker of the California State Assembly (and future mayor of Los Angeles); and Villaraigosa's children and wife, Corina. Proposition 187, approved by California voters in a 1994 ballot initiative, would have denied services such as non-emergency health care and public education to illegal immigrants and their children.

and Senate both considered legislation that would cut the yearly immigration limit by as much as a third. But the bills were defeated in 1996, and the anti-immigrant mood began to wane. Support for immigration had been buoyed by the boom in the economy during the late 1990s, and by June 2001 the proportion of people who said they were happy with the number of immigrants entering (42 percent) was larger than the proportion wanting to scale it back (41 percent). An additional 14 percent—a record high at that time—said the number of immigrants should be increased.

Pro-immigration sentiment changed dramatically after the terrorist attacks of September 11, 2001. One month later Gallup found 58 percent of respondents thought immigration should be cut back, while only 30 percent said the level should stay the same. When the terrorist threat receded in American minds, the pro-immigration numbers began to crawl back up again. In a 2004 Gallup survey, about half (49 percent) wanted less immigration, while the percentage of people who wanted immigration to increase was back up at 14 percent. However, by the following year concerns about illegal immigration were on the rise once again, and a Gallup poll showed most Americans now favored less legal immigration, too.

While the national identities of today's immigrants are different, the anxieties over them are similar to those felt in previous eras: Are today's Hispanic and Asian immigrants taking jobs from Americans? Will the U.S. government apprehend the Islamic radicals intent on doing the nation harm? Can illegal immigration be brought under control? And will most of the millions of newcomers learn English and assimilate?

4

SPEAKING OF LANGUAGE

I n June 1995, Judge Samuel C. Kiser of the Texas District Court in Amarillo ruled that a Mexican immigrant named Martha Laureano was being a bad parent. He compared her practice of speaking only Spanish to her five-year-old daughter to child abuse, and ordered that she speak to the little girl in English only or risk losing custody. The child needed to know English, Judge Kiser ruled; otherwise she was relegating her "to the position of housemaid."

Just about everybody agrees that knowing English is a good thing for someone living in the United States. Kids will not do well in school if they do not know English, nor will they have many good job opportunities when they grow up. But the Texas case raised questions beyond those concerning the obvious benefits of knowing English; during a time of anti-foreigner anxiety, it delved into the controversies surrounding immigration and language. People asked, wouldn't that five-year-old girl learn English anyway, even if her mother continued to talk to her in Spanish? And to what extent should the government regulate language use in

(Opposite) Child abuse? That's how a district judge in Texas characterized Martha Laureano's insistence on speaking only Spanish to her five-year-old daughter, Faviola. A Mexican immigrant, Laureano, seen here with Faviola, wanted the girl to grow up bilingual. Language has often been a trigger for acrimonious debate on the larger questions of immigration and what it means to be an American.

public? What about speaking a different language in a person's own home?

Ever since millions of immigrants started arriving on U.S. shores in the mid-1800s, the country has welcomed people who speak languages other than English. In 1930 the U.S. census tallied 13.9 million people whose mother tongue was not English—at the time a record number. Seventy years later census takers found 47 million people aged five and older who did not speak English at home; 21.3 million of this segment said they spoke English "less than very well."

A Gallup survey in 2001 asked a slightly different question that revealed the impact immigration was having on language use in the United States. It found that 26 percent of American adults spoke a language other than English well enough to hold a conversation. For a majority of these Americans—55 percent—that other language was Spanish. In addition, 17 percent of the survey respondents spoke French, 10 percent spoke German, 3 percent spoke Italian, and 2 percent spoke Chinese.

ENGLISH ONLY, ENGLISH MOSTLY, ENGLISH PLUS

The fact that so many people in the United States regularly use a language other than English is a source of concern to many Americans. This anxiety is behind the battle over language. On one side of the debate people argue that immigration threatens the predominance of English. Their opponents insist that English will always be the primary language of the nation, and that fear of foreign languages is based on nothing more than an irrational fear of immigrants.

Much of the negative sentiment over foreign language use may be shaped by personal encounters people have had with immigrants, according to Gallup. A 1997 survey found that 22 percent of respondents had in the previous year been unable to get what they wanted

Bilingual Ability

"Do you personally speak a language other than English well enough
to hold a conversation?"

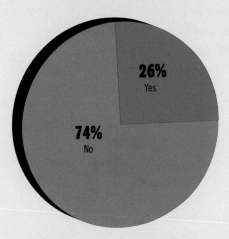

Poll taken March 2001; 1,023 total respondents
Source: The Gallup Organization

"Which foreign language do you speak well enough to hold a conversation?"

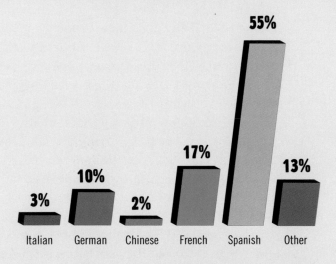

Poll taken March 2001; 265 total respondents
Source: The Gallup Organization

in a store because its employees did not speak English. While not a majority, this figure represents a sizeable percentage for a predominantly English-speaking country. The same survey asked whether businesses should be "required to provide English-language training to immigrants they employ who are not fluent in English." A high proportion—56 percent—of respondents answered yes.

On one side of the language controversy is the movement to make English the official language. Although the country as a whole recognizes no official tongue, at least 27 states and dozens of counties and municipalities have passed laws to make English official. In some of those places government must conduct most business and print the majority of public notices in English only; in others the law is merely a symbolic declaration of English's "official" status.

"English, the greatest unifier in our nation's history, is under assault in our schools, in our courts and by bureaucrats," wrote Mauro Mujica, chairman of U.S. English, a group that promotes making English the official language. "While using a multitude of languages in business, at home or in worship is valuable, it is burdensome, needlessly expensive and inappropriate in government. What's more, it only serves as a disincentive to immigrants to learn English, the language 97 percent of our country speaks."

But if English-only laws are meant to stamp out the use of foreign languages, as Mujica would argue, they have failed. Dade County, Florida, which includes Miami, made English an official language between 1980 and 1993, and in California, English has been official since 1986. However, both places are still home to huge populations of immigrants who know other tongues.

Opponents of the official-language laws believe English is not threatened, and they frequently place pressure on the government to offer certain services in different languages, particularly those services that are required by law. One such service provides bilingual election aids to minority-language speakers. Since 1975, federal law has dictated that in places where more than 10,000, or at least 5 percent, of voting-age citizens are not English proficient, local election officials must provide ballots in the minority language or bilingual assistance in the polling place.

Following the 2000 presidential election, many advocates for the Spanish-speaking community argued that its voting rights had not been protected. Raúl Yzaguirre, president of the civil rights organization National Council of La Raza, brought this claim before the U.S. Senate in 2001. "Every voter has the right to cast an informed and effective vote," he stated. "This right is extended to all people, including those for whom English is not their first language."

BILINGUAL EDUCATION AND ENGLISH IMMERSION

The controversy over language use extends to the classroom. Schools in the United States follow two basic systems of teaching children who do not know English: bilingual education and what has been termed the "immersion" method. In bilingual education, non-English-speaking students spend part of the school day in special classrooms where they learn how to speak English, and the rest of the day taking other subjects (such as math, science, or history), which are taught in their native languages. The immersion method requires that all instruction be in English.

The argument in favor of bilingual education is that while students learn English, they also keep up to grade level in the other subjects by attending classes taught in a language they understand. Without bilingual education, proponents contend, children are forced to sit in history or mathematics classes where they cannot understand the teacher and inevitably fall behind in those subjects.

Supporters of immersion disagree. They say children can learn very quickly, especially when they attend classes taught only in English. Newer immersion programs also make sure that students briefly run through the basics of English before venturing into other subjects. "The English immersion program that we use doesn't just throw non-English speaking children into English-only classrooms," writes Kenneth Noonan, superintendent of Oceanside Unified School District in California. "In our program, the first year in immersion is focused on acquiring basic English language skills. . . . As the students reach a certain level of English proficiency, they begin to apply it to academic content areas."

Scholars remain divided about whether bilingual education or the English immersion method is more efficient. Gallup polls indicate that ordinary Americans favor immersion over bilingual education. In 1993 only 27 percent of respondents supported bilingual education, while 46 percent believed immersion was the best option. Nearly a quarter said parents should be required to pay out of their own pockets for English classes before public schools allowed their children to enroll.

In 1998 California, which has one of the highest percentages of immigrant students who do not know English, became the first state in the nation to do away with bilingual education. Shortly after the decision a Gallup poll found that Americans in general supported the California measure: 63 percent preferred immersion, while just 34 percent favored bilingual instruction.

By 2003, however, the country seemed more open to bilingual instruction. In a Gallup poll that year 58 percent of respondents said schools should offer bilingual classes, while 40 percent said such classes should not be offered—almost the reverse of what Americans thought in 1998. The poll also found differences in the way people of different ethnic backgrounds saw the issue. Most notably, 72 percent of Hispanics favored bilingual education, compared with 53 percent of non-Hispanic whites. This finding was no surprise, as many Spanish-speaking parents, like their German counterparts more than a century before, see no problem with their kids spending part of the school day learning history or math in the language of their home country.

The 2003 poll also recorded people's responses by their party affiliation: 69 percent of Democrats favored bilingual education, while 46 percent of Republicans favored immersion, a result underlining the political reality that liberals tend to favor bilingual education while conservatives generally oppose it. "The gap between Republicans and Democrats on this question is

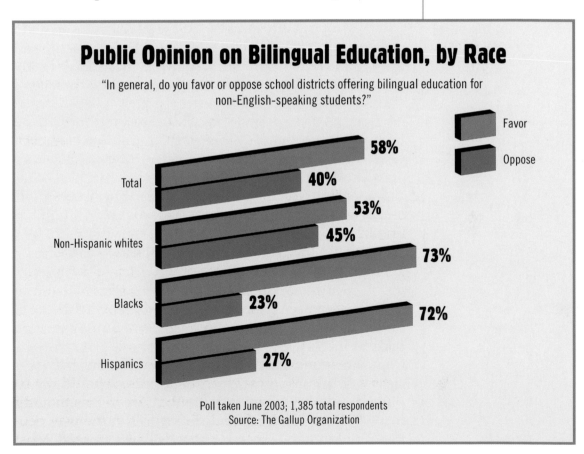

Public Opinion on Bilingual Education, by Race

"In general, do you favor or oppose school districts offering bilingual education for non-English-speaking students?"

Favor

Oppose

Total: 58% / 40%

Non-Hispanic whites: 53% / 45%

Blacks: 73% / 23%

Hispanics: 72% / 27%

Poll taken June 2003; 1,385 total respondents
Source: The Gallup Organization

somewhat larger than the gaps among whites, Hispanics, and blacks," Gallup contributing editor Heather Mason noted.

WHEN WILL THEY EVER LEARN?

Today's anxieties over whether immigrants will ever speak English hark back to the same anxieties Americans felt a century ago. "The ultimate way to bring this nation to ruin, or preventing all possibility of it continuing to be a nation at all, would be to permit it to become a tangle of squabbling nationalities," said Theodore Roosevelt, U.S. president between 1901 and 1909. "We have but one flag; we must also learn one language, and that language is English." Such concerns were backed up by the federal Dillingham Commission study, a report published in 1911 that was filled with cultural prejudices. It accused Italian, Slavic, and Jewish immigrants of failing to learn English as quickly as the Germans and Scandinavians who preceded them.

Despite the worries voiced during that time, many immigrants and many more of their children eventually learned English. Today few of their descendants can speak their ancestral language. English is the mother tongue of nearly all the descendants of Italian, Slavic, and Jewish immigrants of the early 1900s. Will the latest wave of immigrants learn too?

Mauro Mujica is not so sure. "Using scare tactics and divisive rhetoric, self-appointed leaders of immigrant groups are trying to prevent newcomers from learning our shared language," he wrote. "This vocal minority wrongly claims that an immigrant's culture and heritage will be lost if he or she agrees to have English as the official language." Others disagree. They say that immigrants are generally eager to learn English, although it takes time for them to become proficient, a fact that many opponents of immigration fail to acknowledge. The reason the 2000 U.S. census found more than 7.6 million people who did not know English well is that most of those individuals were immigrants who had not been in the United States long enough to learn the language. "Immigrants traditionally have learned enough English to get by," author James Crawford wrote in *Hold Your Tongue: Bilingualism and the Politics of "English Only."* "[T]heir children have become bilingual, using the ethnic language less as they grow older; and the grandchildren have been raised largely as monolingual English speakers."

One study conducted by Richard Alba, sociology professor at the State University of New York at Albany, suggests Crawford may be right. Using data from the 2000 census, he concluded that among nearly every major immigrant group, 90 percent of the U.S.-born children speak English well. He also found that among members of the third generation—the children of the U.S.-born children—use of the old language tended to disappear entirely. Ninety-two percent of third-generation Asian Americans and 71 percent of third-generation Hispanics spoke only English at home, and among the one-quarter or so living in bilingual households, nearly all spoke English well. "English is almost universally accepted by the children and grandchildren of the immigrants who have come to the U.S. in great numbers since the 1960s, which means these children have high levels of linguistic assimilation," concluded Alba. "[B]y the third generation, only a minority in any group maintains bilingualism."

Studies like that done by Alba indicate that, like the descendants of 19th- and early-20th-century immigrants, the children and grandchildren of today's immigrants will probably also leave their ancestral tongue behind. Such studies support the conclusion that what is threatened is not the predominance of English but the survival of immigrant languages.

5

HELP WANTED

Every weekday beginning at 7 A.M. immigrant job seekers jam the dingy waiting room of the Atlas Employment Agency in New York, looking for work washing dishes and clearing tables in one of the city's restaurants. "Busboy, rápido," agency owner Dinos Kazanis shouts to the crowd of applicants one morning, as the *New York Times* described the scene. A young man named Rodolfo, who arrived from Mexico less than a year before, stands up and Kazanis gives him the job. It pays $500 for a 50-hour week, there are no health benefits, and the agency will bill Rodolfo $100 for finding him employment.

A very small paycheck by U.S. standards. But it is more than Rodolfo would have earned in Mexico for a similar job, had he been lucky enough to find one. These days, the *Times* story explained, most job seekers at Atlas are Mexican. When Kazanis, who emigrated from Greece in the 1980s, first opened for business, most applicants were from Bangladesh or China. Like the Italians, Jews, and Irish who preceded these groups, today's newcomers come to

(Opposite) This sign on the window of a job placement company in a suburb of Chicago attests to the growing role of Latino immigrants, particularly Mexicans, in the U.S. labor force. In many parts of the country, the hotel, restaurant, commercial housekeeping, and construction industries could not function without immigrant workers.

the United States seeking opportunities they could not find in their native lands.

The job-seeking immigrants at the Atlas agency have little education and take work that pays little, requires few skills, and carries no prestige. Many others are in the same shoes. According to a report by the American Immigration Law Foundation, immigrants who arrived in the 1990s make up 153,000 of the nation's janitors, 162,000 of the agricultural workers, and 194,000 of the cooks. However, other immigrants are highly educated

Given the bleak economic prospects in their homelands, many immigrants from impoverished countries are willing to accept low-wage, physically grueling jobs in the United States—and many employers are happy to hire them. Some labor leaders and politicians charge that high levels of immigration (especially illegal immigration) thus have the effect of depressing the wages of American workers, and even of taking jobs away from native-born Americans. Immigrant advocates counter that Americans aren't willing to do the low-end jobs that immigrants accept.

professionals who left their homelands in the belief that the entrepreneur-driven U.S. economy would give them the greatest chance to do their best work. The National Immigration Forum (NIF)—an organization based in Washington, D.C., that promotes the benefits of immigration—says that 51 percent of engineers who hold a doctorate degree in the United States are foreign-born. They are part of an old immigrant tradition: just as the 19th-century Scottish immigrant Alexander Graham Bell invented the telephone, Hungarian-born Andy Grove built up Intel Corporation to become the world's largest manufacturer of computer chips.

Immigrants like Andy Grove have revolutionized the high-technology sector. Their influence has been particularly profound on California's Silicon Valley, the heart of the American computer industry. Software and hardware companies founded by Indian or Chinese immigrants there generated more than $19.5 billion in sales and nearly 73,000 jobs in 2000, according to the NIF.

The great success that some immigrants enjoy attracts a certain degree of scrutiny, as do the foreign laborers willing to work for very low wages in the United States. Are they taking Americans' jobs, or creating jobs for them? Are they paying into the system with their taxes, or draining it by consuming too many government services?

WHOSE JOBS?

"NATIVES OF THE SOIL! AROUSE! Shall American Labor Be Protected Against Foreign Competition in the Home Labor Market?" Those were the screaming headlines in a flyer for one of the speeches given by Foster Bryant, an attorney who traveled through U.S. cities during the 19th century to denounce what he called the "ruinous influence of foreign immigration on American labor." More than 100 years later, Americans are still vocal about immigration. The rhetoric is now toned down and more sophisticated among those pushing for decreased immigration, but the message is still the same: immigrants take jobs from Americans.

Steven A. Camarota, research director of the Center for Immigration Studies (CIS), an organization that calls for lower rates of immigration, says that even though the number of adults working in the United States increased between 2000 and 2004, immigrant workers benefited the most from the job growth. "While the number of unemployed adult native-born workers increased by 2.3 million over this time, the number of employed immigrants rose by 2.3 million," Camarota wrote.

Other experts, such as those affiliated with the NIF and the American Immigration Law Foundation (AILF), reach the opposite conclusion. "The notion that every job filled by an immigrant is one less job available for a native-born worker is inherently simplistic and doesn't account for the fact that immigrants create jobs or that unemployed natives and immigrant workers often do not compete for the same jobs," wrote researcher Robert Paral in an AILF report.

A key component of the anti-immigration perspective is the argument that newcomers work for less money than native-born Americans and thus depress wages for everybody. A study conducted by Harvard economist George Borjas for the CIS concluded that between 1980 and 2000 "immigration reduced the average annual earnings of native-born men by $1,700, or roughly 4 percent." According to the study, the impact was larger among those without a high school education, who saw their earnings reduced by 7.4 percent because of immigration.

Camarota believes much of the immigration problem lies in letting American employers have unfair wage policies. "When businesses say, 'Immigrants only take jobs Americans don't want,' what they really mean is that given what they would like to pay, and how they would like to treat their workers, they cannot find enough Americans," he wrote. "Therefore, employers want the government to continually increase the supply of labor by nonenforcement of immigration laws and keeping legal immigration levels as high as possible. This in turn holds down wages and benefits, especially at the bottom end of the labor market."

Immigration advocates argue that an interpretation like Camarota's fails to recognize the contributions from the many immigrants who are entrepreneurs and academics. "Immigrant entrepreneurs create jobs for U.S. and foreign workers, and foreign-born students allow many U.S. graduate programs to keep their doors open," says the Brookings Institution, an independent think tank. The pro-immigration side asserts that the focus must always remain on the total economic output of immigrants. "[D]istinguishing between jobs merely on the basis of whether they are held by natives or immigrants," Robert Paral writes, "ignores the fact that many 'native' jobs are in immigrant-owned businesses, or are made possible by the purchasing power of immigrants."

The American public seems to be of two minds about the controversy, Gallup surveys show. Polls taken in 2001, 2002, and 2004 show that roughly half of Americans believe immigration has no significant impact on jobs. However, among the remaining half, a solid majority believes immigration's impact is negative. The polls asked respondents to rate the impact immigrants were having on several aspects of American life. When asked about immigration's impact on job opportunities, 51 percent of the 2004 survey's respondents said immigrants did not have much effect, but 37 percent said they made things worse and just 11 percent said immigrants made the situation better.

Although a large majority of respondents said immigrants take jobs native-born Americans do not want, 65 percent also agreed with the statement that immigrants "mostly hurt the economy by driving down wages for many Americans." These results represented a decline in support for immigration over the previous four years: in a 2000 poll, during a time of economic health and relatively good feelings toward immigration, more respondents said immigrants helped by providing cheap labor (44 percent) than they hurt by lowering wages (40 percent).

TAXING SERVICES

Another question about the economic impact of immigration focuses on taxes and government services. Proponents of immigration contend that immigrants produce a net gain for the Treasury, paying more in taxes than they use in social services. Opponents of immigration say the opposite—that immigrants represent a drain on the economy because they earn less money than the average worker, pay little in taxes, and overuse government services.

Those holding the latter view counted as a victory President Bill Clinton's 1996 signing of a landmark welfare reform bill. The legislation barred most legal immigrants from obtaining food stamps and Supplemental Security Income (SSI). It also established that future immigrants would have to wait five years before becoming eligible for most federal aid programs for the poor. As a result, some 935,000 non-citizens lost their benefits, according to the AILF.

A CNN/USA Today/Gallup poll taken two years before the welfare bill was passed indicated that Americans supported such a measure. Respondents were asked which of the following two statements represented their point of view: "immigrants cost the taxpayers too much by using government services like public education and medical services," or "immigrants in the long run become productive citizens and pay their fair share of taxes." A solid majority (nearly 57 percent) agreed with the former statement, while only 36 percent agreed with the latter. When they were asked about a measure to "eliminate all forms of public assistance, including education and health benefits, to all legal immigrants and their children," just 24 percent of respondents said they would favor it, while nearly three-quarters (73 percent) were opposed.

Over the years that followed, the United States restored many of the benefits that it denied immigrants. A 2003 report by the CIS says that immigrants today are

President Bill Clinton signs a welfare reform bill in a Rose Garden ceremony, August 21, 1996. The controversial legislation not only barred most legal immigrants from collecting welfare benefits such as food stamps and Supplemental Security Income (cash assistance for the blind, disabled, and elderly) but also specified that future immigrants would have to wait five years before becoming eligible for most federal aid programs for the poor.

more likely to receive government aid than native-born Americans. It found that more than 25.5 percent of immigrant households receive some form of welfare benefits (such as direct payment to families, food stamps, or housing subsidies), compared with 16.7 percent of native households. The rival NIF contests the CIS claim that immigrants do not contribute their share of tax revenue. "The ratio between immigrant use of public benefits and the amount of taxes they pay is consistently favorable to the U.S.," asserts the NIF. "Immigrants earn about $240 billion a year, pay about $90 billion a year in taxes, and use about $5 billion in public benefits."

How can these two groups reach contradictory results on the same issue? One answer is that they are selective in choosing the statistics that support their argument. In the case above, the CIS, an organization fighting for decreased immigration, used data reported by individual households, while the pro-immigration NIF focused on total national revenue and expenses.

Since 2000, the Gallup polls have suggested that about half of Americans would agree with the stance of the CIS and other organizations favoring lower immigration. In 2000, for example, 46 percent said that immigration has a bad effect on taxes; that figure jumped to 50 percent in the 2002 survey, then dropped down to 45 percent in 2004. In each of the polls, a consistent 12 percent told pollsters that immigration makes the tax picture better.

That last figure may increase in the years ahead if, as immigration proponents anticipate, the growing numbers of immigrants help save the country's Social Security system from a looming crisis. Social Security — which pays benefits to retirees as well as the disabled and minor children of deceased parents — is funded by a payroll tax paid by current workers and their employers. Because the giant segment of the U.S. population known as the baby boomer generation is nearing retirement age and there will be fewer active workers to pay into the system, the Social Security Trust Fund is projected to face a growing shortfall over the coming decades. Tax-paying immigrants could contribute enough to pay the balance, says the National Foundation for American Policy. The organization projects that "over the next 75 years, new legal immigrants entering the United States will provide a net benefit of $611 billion" to the Social Security system.

In the years ahead, it is likely that pro- and anti-immigration groups will continue to clash over how immigration affects the job market, taxes, and Social Security. One thing for sure is that the U.S. economy is large and dynamic enough to continue making room for immigrants, even if newcomers struggle when they first arrive.

6

ILLEGAL IMMIGRATION

Jesús Alonzo Camacho stood on the porch of a house in Las Chepas, Mexico, just across the U.S. border from New Mexico, trying to figure out a way into the United States. "We can't support ourselves at home," the 44-year-old Mexican farmer, who earns around six dollars a day working the fields in his home state of Michoacán, told the *Washington Post*. "We need the money from the other side."

Plenty of jobs await the millions who illegally cross to "the other side," even in places where few immigrants are settled. There are suburban lawns to be mowed, restaurants' dishes to be washed, leaky roofs to be sealed. Employers hire illegal immigrants because they work for less money than Americans or even legal immigrants. And the workers take the illegal jobs because they earn more than they would in their countries of origin. Yet the road to better employment is filled with significant obstacles, as the *Washington Post* reported:

> Facing Camacho and the others across a near-by ditch was an astounding high-tech spider-web spun by the U.S. Border Patrol in New

(Opposite) Illegal immigrants scale a fence separating Agua Prieta, Mexico, from Douglas, Arizona. Each day thousands of Mexicans, Central Americans, and others try to sneak across the 2,000-mile U.S.-Mexico border, much of which runs across remote, sparsely populated areas.

73

Mexico. Motion sensors were buried in the ground. High-resolution infrared cameras were mounted on poles, able to spot people five miles off. A man hiding in the dark would pop up larger than life on video monitors 35 miles away, so detailed that technicians could see him sneeze.

On the ground, agents in big sport-utility vehicles were armed with night-vision goggles and satellite global positioning devices. Helicopters buzzed up and down the border, shining powerful spotlights. U.S. Army units preparing to head for Iraq were holding exercises here, catching illegal immigrants with precision surveillance equipment designed for war.

While the U.S. government mounts its huge effort to stop people from entering the country illegally, many American employers continually show their eagerness to give them jobs—a reminder of the complicated and even contradictory relationship between the United States and its illegal immigrants. On the one hand, Americans believe that one of government's highest priorities in a post-9/11 world is to protect the borders so that terrorists do not enter the United States, and that immigration law should be enforced like any other law. In keeping with this view, three-quarters of respondents (74 percent) to a 2004 Gallup poll believed the government should not change the law to make it easier for illegal immigrants to become U.S. citizens.

However, along with the push for tighter borders comes the temptation to hire people who will work for less than others, which of course results in greater numbers of illegal immigrants. Many who try to slip into the country without the proper authorization are stopped. Officials made some 1.1 million apprehensions on the border in 2004, a 24 percent increase over 2003. It is hard to determine whether the increase reflects a jump in the number of illegal immigrants trying to get into the United States or an improvement of law enforcement's performance in catching them. What is known is that a lot of illegal immigrants still make it through.

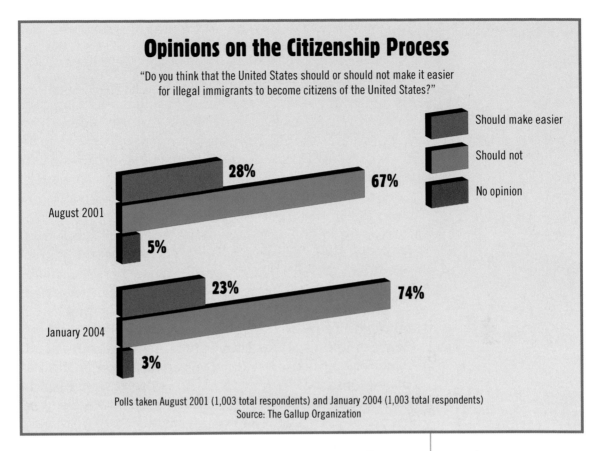

Opinions on the Citizenship Process

"Do you think that the United States should or should not make it easier
for illegal immigrants to become citizens of the United States?"

Should make easier

Should not

No opinion

August 2001
28%
67%
5%

January 2004
23%
74%
3%

Polls taken August 2001 (1,003 total respondents) and January 2004 (1,003 total respondents)
Source: The Gallup Organization

According to an estimate by the Pew Hispanic Center, in 2004 there were 11 million illegal immigrants living in the United States, 6 million of whom were Mexicans. They made up 29 percent of all the foreign-born people living in the United States that year.

WE HAVE A PROBLEM

As an issue of national concern, illegal immigration received comparatively little attention through the 1960s and 1970s, even though significant numbers of undocumented migrants began crossing the border from Mexico in the wake of the Immigration and Nationality Act of 1965, which imposed a cap on the total number of immigrants who could be admitted annually from the Western Hemisphere. (Before this time, numerical restrictions on immigration did not affect countries in the Western Hemisphere.) By the early 1980s, however, Americans had begun to acknowledge that illegal immigration was a problem that had to be dealt with. In 1982 a Gallup poll asked about support for a law making it illegal "to hire an immigrant who has come into the U.S. without proper papers." Nearly 65 percent of respondents to the poll said they would support such a law, while 32 percent said they would not. Other surveys over the next couple of years revealed the extent of Americans' concerns as an increasing number of illegal immigrants arrived and the issue became more prominent. The country began to wrestle more with questions about illegal immigration.

In another Gallup poll, taken in 1984, Americans showed they wanted their government to crack down on illegal immigration. More than half of the respondents (55 percent) said that illegal immigrants should be deported, while a little less than 35 percent said that they should be given amnesty. In addition, 61 percent of respondents favored penalties for employers who knowingly hired illegal immigrants; only 28 percent opposed such penalties.

Yet at the same time, Americans seemed to have no illusions that implementing stronger security measures would solve the problem of illegal immigration. Gallup pollsters found that 60 percent of respondents opposed "spending more in money and manpower to patrol our borders" because it would be too expensive and would not work. O ne-third (33 percent) of respondents wanted border security beefed up. Still, 55 percent said illegal immigration was a "very important problem" in a 1984 poll, and two years later, 40 percent of respondents told Gallup that the otherwise hugely popular President Ronald Reagan was doing a poor job handling illegal immigration.

It was during that same year that the government tried to tackle the growing crisis with the Immigration

Amnesty or Arrest?

"Some people say that there are too many illegal immigrants living in this country for the authorities to arrest and deport them. They feel we should have an amnesty to let most of them live here legally. Others say that the government should do everything it can to arrest and deport those living in this country illegally. Which view comes closer to your own?"

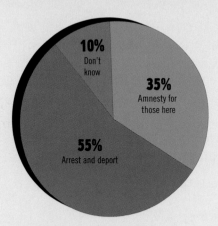

10%
Don't
know

35%
Amnesty for
those here

55%
Arrest and deport

Poll taken June 1984; 1,258 total respondents
Source: The Gallup Organization

Immigrant Employment and Penalties

"Some people say the government should make it much more difficult for illegal aliens to get work in the U.S. by penalizing companies that knowingly hire them. Others oppose such a penalty because it would restrict U.S. businesses too much and limit opportunities for legal immigrants, especially Hispanics. Which view comes closer to your own?"

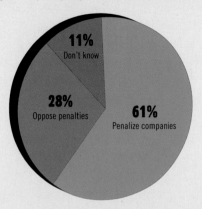

11%
Don't know

28%
Oppose penalties

61%
Penalize companies

Poll taken June 1984; 1,258 total respondents
Source: The Gallup Organization

Reform and Control Act (IRCA) of 1986. Despite public sentiment against issuing amnesty to people in the country illegally, IRCA legalized the status of some 2.7 million illegal immigrants who had immigrated to the United States before 1982 or had done farm work for a minimum of 90 days before the law was passed. Immigration authorities believed that these conditions covered most of the illegal immigrants then living on U.S. soil. To prevent more from entering, IRCA also increased border enforcement and created sanctions for employers who hired illegal immigrants. The intention was to let those who were already in the country stay, while at the same time discouraging or preventing any more from arriving.

THE ANGRY MID-'90S

But IRCA did not solve the problem. Illegal immigrants continued to come and find work despite increased border patrols and employer sanctions. People also found that sneaking across the border was not the only way to enter the United States—a significant number of illegal immigrants arrived legally on temporary visas and simply stayed after the permit expired. Immigration and law enforcement officials did not have the resources to ensure that all the millions of foreign tourists, students, business travelers, temporary workers, and others who entered the country each year actually left when they were supposed to.

After IRCA was passed, some employers in high positions found themselves the target of investigations regarding their hiring practices. Even close associates of the U.S. president attracted controversy. In 1993 the newly elected Bill Clinton nominated Zoe Baird for attorney general, but she withdrew her nomination after newspapers reported that she and her husband had hired an illegal immigrant to be their babysitter. A Gallup poll showed how intensely the public felt about this issue when it found 63 percent of Americans believed the U.S. Senate should not confirm Baird as the nation's highest law enforcement officer. Amazingly enough, Clinton's next nominee for attorney general, Kimba Wood, faced a similar controversy for hiring an illegal immigrant. The difference between the two cases was that Wood had hired an illegal immigrant to work in her home before the passage of IRCA. Nonetheless, Wood, like Baird, ultimately was compelled to withdraw her nomination.

Illegal immigration was a hot issue during this time. Although Proposition 187—which sought to prohibit all forms of government services to illegal immigrants in California—never became law, the debate did not go away after it was ruled unconstitutional in 1995. That year Gallup asked people throughout the nation if they

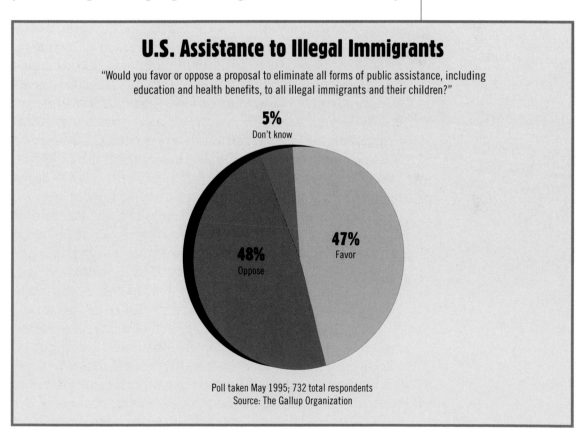

U.S. Assistance to Illegal Immigrants

"Would you favor or oppose a proposal to eliminate all forms of public assistance, including education and health benefits, to all illegal immigrants and their children?"

5%
Don't know

48%
Oppose

47%
Favor

Poll taken May 1995; 732 total respondents
Source: The Gallup Organization

would "favor or oppose a proposal to eliminate all forms of public assistance, including education and health benefits, to all illegal immigrants and their children." The response was evenly divided: 47 percent said they would favor such a proposal, and 48 percent said they would oppose it. About 5 percent weren't sure. When, in a 2004 survey, Gallup pollsters asked non-Californians whether they would like a law similar to Proposition 187 in their state, 63 percent said yes, while 34 percent said no. Interestingly, Californians were much more closely divided on the issue, with 53 percent of respondents in favor of eliminating benefits for illegal immigrants and 47 percent opposed.

A SHORT CALM

Despite the furor of the mid-1990s, immigration became a less contentious issue for Americans as the decade wore on, particularly during the economic boom of the late 1990s. Nonetheless, anxieties about illegal immigration remained. In August 2001, two-thirds of respondents told Gallup pollsters that the United States should not make it easier for illegal immigrants to become citizens. However, those same anxieties did not extend to legal immigration: in a survey taken in June of that year, 62 percent of respondents said immigration was "a good thing for the country."

Four months later, in December 2001, 58 percent of Americans told Gallup that immigration should be reduced. What happened to cause the change? The terrorist attacks of September 11, 2001. Worried about security, the American public wanted fewer people allowed in. Fears about terrorism re-ignited the immigration issue. But this time, unlike during the 1990s, there was no widely supported legislation in Congress to cut immigrants' benefits or lower the number of legal immigrants permitted to enter. Some political observers traced the reluctance to pursue this agenda to the growing influence of Hispanics, more than 40 percent of whom voted for George W. Bush in the 2004 presidential election, the highest ever for a Republican candidate. With legal immigration less of an issue, attention turned to securing the borders and dealing with the continued escalation in illegal immigration.

Critics said the federal government was not doing enough to guard the nation's borders. Seeing an opportunity to address the problem, an 800-strong civilian patrol that called itself the Minutemen spent the month of April 2005 guarding a 23-mile sector of the San Pedro Valley, on the border between Arizona and Mexico, where 40 percent of the Border Patrol's illegal-immigrant apprehensions were taking place. The Border

Advocates for migrants protest the activities of the California Border Watch, July 20, 2005. Like the Arizona-based Minutemen, the California Border Watch is composed of civilian volunteers who monitor areas near the Mexico border to detect, and alert U.S. Border Patrol agents to, illegal immigrants.

Patrol officially disowned the group, whose members President Bush referred to as "vigilantes." Yet the Minutemen, some of whom carried firearms during their patrols, received support from certain conservative activists, as well as California governor Arnold Schwarzenegger.

Did the Minutemen do a better job than the Border Patrol in slowing illegal immigration? In April 2004 the Border Patrol caught more than 64,000 illegal immigrants in the same sector; in April 2005, as the Minutemen conducted their patrols, arrests went down to 5,000. The Minutemen said the lower arrest figures showed that many fewer people attempted to cross illegally while they were patrolling, and that the Border Patrol could achieve similar results if it increased its manpower. Pro-immigrant groups, however, argued that merely beefing up border security was a short-term approach that did not address the larger issue. "Many involved with the Minuteman Project and the broader anti-immigration movement feel we cannot consider reforming immigration until we get control of our borders, but that is precisely backwards," the NIF said. "We cannot get control of our borders until we reform our immigration laws so that they match more closely with reality. Reformed laws must meet the needs of employers, immigrants, and this nation's citizens."

The Bush administration seemed to agree with this perspective. In early 2004, more than a year before the Minutemen appeared on the scene, the president presented a plan to allow some illegal immigrants to stay in the United States. Bush proposed that if illegal immigrants had employers who were willing to sponsor them—in jobs Americans did not want—they should be permitted to apply for temporary worker status and apply for permanent residency later. The plan stipulated that if illegal immigrants wanted to get that residence permit, they would have to wait in line behind immigrants who used legal channels. Those not granted residency would be deported.

Although some of the details of the president's plan were not well received by Congress, the central premise garnered considerable support. In May 2005, Senators John McCain, a Republican from Arizona, and Edward M. Kennedy, a Democrat from Massachusetts, introduced the Secure America and Orderly Immigration Act. The bill stipulated that illegal immigrants who paid back taxes plus a $2,000 fee and underwent a background check would be permitted to stay and work for six years. At the end of that period, they would either have to return to their country of origin or apply for permanent residency. To become legal residents, illegal immigrants would need to have a job and show that

Senator John McCain of Arizona (left) confers with his colleague, Senator Edward Kennedy of Massachusetts. In May 2005 the two senators introduced the Secure America and Orderly Immigration Act.

they were learning English. The bill also called for 400,000 new visas for people who wanted to enter the United States and had secured a job requiring little or no skills.

Opponents of the legislation said the McCain-Kennedy bill, like the Bush proposal a year earlier, amounted to providing amnesty for illegal immigrants. The public was split on the issue. In a Gallup poll taken one month after Bush presented his plan, more Americans opposed than favored the proposal (51 percent versus 46 percent). The results reflected the difficulties of dealing with illegal immigration.

As a practical matter, apprehending and deporting more than 11 million individuals would present an impossible task for U.S. law enforcement. But beyond that, immigrant advocates say it is not fair to expel illegal immigrant families who have been in the country for a decade or more working hard, staying out of trouble, and bringing up children who know only life in the United States. Still, other Americans insist deportation is the proper punishment for people who break immigration law.

Then there is the question of how to stop more illegal immigrants from coming. It seems likely that, as long as there are insufficient employment opportunities in their home countries, people will continue to cross the border into the United States—whatever way they can—in order to find jobs to support themselves and their families. One response to the problem, which the McCain-Kennedy bill sought to employ, would be to increase the number of immigrants allowed to enter the country legally under work visas. In theory, this would present economic migrants with an attractive alternative to entering the country illegally—but it remained an open question whether enough visas would be made available to fill the enormous demand, or whether immigrants would want to abide by various conditions imposed under the temporary visas. Another response (not mutually exclusive with the above measure) would be to put more guards on the borders.

Since the attacks of September 11, 2001, immigration policy has become a much more urgent issue for Americans, regardless of their political viewpoint. Everyone agrees that whatever new policies are crafted, they must address the kinds of security vulnerabilities exposed by the 19 foreign-born hijackers.

TERRORISTS OR IMMIGRANTS?

Two weeks after the terrorist attacks of September 11, 2001, a 51-year-old Arab immigrant from Yemen named Abdo Ali Ahmed found a note on his car windshield that said, "We're going to kill all of you [expletive] Arabs." Ahmed, an employee of a convenience store in Reedley, California, threw the note away without notifying police. Two days later, he was shot to death at his store.

The murder of Ahmed was part of the post-9/11 wave of hate crimes against Muslim and Arab immigrants, which according to FBI statistics increased 1,700 percent in 2001. There were beatings, threats against mosques, and even cases of arson. Citing a study by a group called South Asian American Leaders of Tomorrow, Human Rights Watch reported that there were 104 bias incidents against places of worship during the first week after September 11. The civil rights group Council on American-Islamic Relations (CAIR) said that in 2004 it processed a record 1,522 incidents of harassment, violence, and discriminatory treatment, a 49 percent increase from the previous year.

(Opposite) Sikh children in Santa Ana, California, attend a memorial service for the victims of the September 11 terrorist attacks, October 10, 2001. In the aftermath of 9/11, Sikhs were targeted in a handful of hate crimes—despite the fact that Sikhs are neither Arab nor Muslim (as were the terrorist hijackers).

ANTI-ARAB FEELINGS

Some 1.2 million persons of Arab ancestry were living in the United States in 2000, according to the Census Bureau. In the 10-year period 1993–2003, more than 290,000 Arabs immigrated to the United States.

Some Americans mistakenly assume that all Arab immigrants hold fundamentalist Islamic beliefs. In fact, a majority of Arabs are not radicals, and some are not even Muslims. Relations between Muslim immigrants and other Americans were already strained before the September 11 attacks. Arabs ranked among the least liked of immigrants, and in a pre-9/11 poll asking people their opinion of 26 different countries and governments, the four lowest rated were predominantly Islamic: the Palestinian Authority, Iran, Libya, and Iraq.

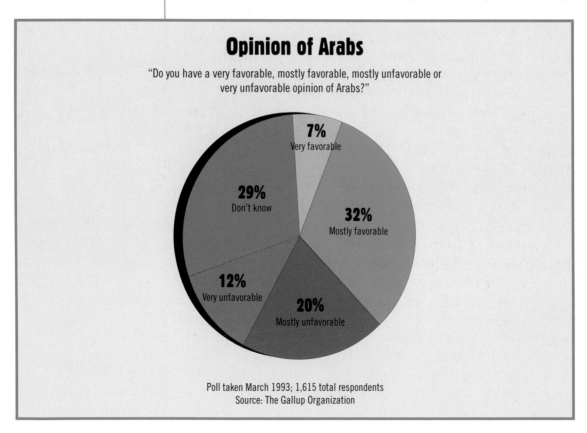

Opinion of Arabs

"Do you have a very favorable, mostly favorable, mostly unfavorable or very unfavorable opinion of Arabs?"

7%
Very favorable

29%
Don't know

32%
Mostly favorable

12%
Very unfavorable

20%
Mostly unfavorable

Poll taken March 1993; 1,615 total respondents
Source: The Gallup Organization

Of these, all but Iran are also Arab. The attitudes of some Americans were affected by the first bombing of the World Trade Center in February 1993—also carried out by Islamist terrorists—which killed six people and injured over a thousand others. A Gallup poll taken a month after the attack showed that just 39 percent of Americans had a favorable opinion of Arabs, while 32 percent had an unfavorable opinion. That same year, near the height of the decade's strongest anti-immigrant feelings, Gallup also found 62 percent of Americans believed that there were "too many" immigrants from Arab countries. That was the highest negative rating for immigrants from any area of the world (including Latin America, a region that sent far more immigrants to the United States).

After airplanes commandeered by Muslim hijackers slammed into the Twin Towers and the Pentagon, American views of Arabs sank even further. In a poll taken three days after the 2001 attacks, Gallup found that "about one in three Americans say that since the attacks, they have heard friends, neighbors, co-workers or acquaintances make negative comments about Arabs living in this country." Yet not all results in that survey were negative for Arabs. A large proportion of respondents, 63 percent, said the attacks did not change the level of trust they had in Arabs living in the United States, while only 35 percent said the attacks made them have less trust.

Personal bias was not the only problem Arab immigrants faced in the wake of the attacks. CAIR reported that the greatest increase in complaints dealt with oppressive law enforcement measures such as "unreasonable arrests, detentions, searches/seizures, and interrogations." In 2004, CAIR said, accusations of this nature accounted for 26 percent of all reported incidents, compared with only 7 percent in 2003. Gallup found that many Americans supported the scrutiny Arab immigrants received from law enforcement agencies. A

September 2001 poll reported that nearly 6 in 10 respondents favored requiring Arabs to undergo more intensive security checks when flying on American airplanes.

THE NEW NORMAL

The 9/11 attacks affected not only attitudes toward Arab and Muslim immigrants, but also policies regarding all immigrants, particularly the several million Mexicans in the country illegally. In the days leading up to September 11, 2001, an immigration reform bill giving legal status to some illegal immigrants seemed inevitable, if not imminent. President Bush had recently said that no foreign nation was more important to the United States than Mexico, and Mexican president Vicente Fox spent part of that first week of September in Washington, D.C., as the Bush administration's first official state visitor. "[W]e must and we can reach an agreement on migration before the end of this very year," Fox said from the South Lawn of the White House, "which will allow us, before the end of our respective terms, to make sure that there are no Mexicans who have not entered this country legally . . . and that those Mexicans who have come into the country do so with the proper documents."

Some political observers believed that even if Fox's predictions seemed too optimistic, some sort of reform on terms close to what the Mexican president sought would come sooner or later. But the plan to reform immigration, like so many other things, came crashing down on the awful morning of September 11.

The weeks and months that followed were a jittery time in U.S. history. In October 85 percent of respondents in a Gallup poll said another terrorist attack was "very likely" or "somewhat likely" in the near future. Yet, over time the public slowly started getting used to what some called "the new normal"—that is, Americans in general began to worry less about an imminent terrorist attack, but still felt less safe than before 9/11.

Negative Comments About Arabs

"Have you personally heard any of your friends, neighbors, fellow workers, or acquaintances make negative comments about Arabs living in this country since the terrorist attacks of 9/11?"

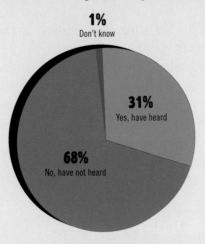

1%
Don't know

31%
Yes, have heard

68%
No, have not heard

Poll taken September 2001; 508 total respondents
Source: The Gallup Organization

Post-9/11 Trust in Arabs

"Would you say that you now have less trust in Arabs living in this country than you did before the terrorist attacks on Tuesday, or has your trust in Arabs living in this country not changed?"

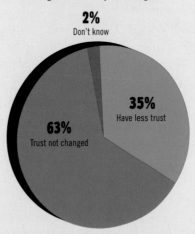

2%
Don't know

35%
Have less trust

63%
Trust not changed

Poll taken September 2001; 524 total respondents
Source: The Gallup Organization

This new attitude became evident as early as a Gallup poll taken in March 2002, just five months after the attacks, when the proportion of respondents who believed another terrorist attack was "very likely" or "somewhat likely" dipped to 52 percent. That would have been an unthinkably high response before 9/11, but it was still a dramatic drop from the 85 percent who said the same thing during the month after the attacks. The number of those who feared an attack rose and fell over the next couple of years. It reached 73 percent when the invasion of Iraq started in March 2003, and dipped to 34 percent in January 2005, after fears of an attack to disrupt the presidential election of 2004 proved unfounded.

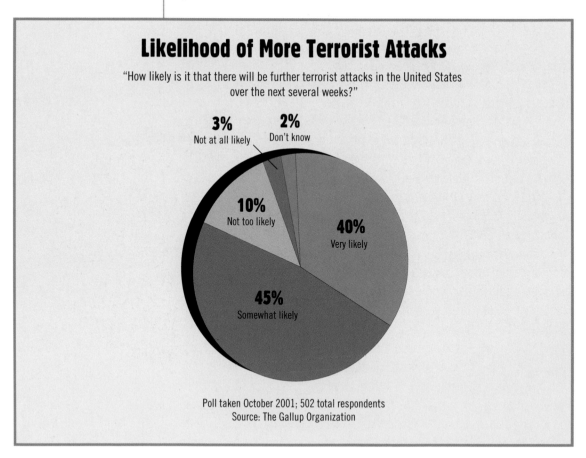

Likelihood of More Terrorist Attacks

"How likely is it that there will be further terrorist attacks in the United States over the next several weeks?"

3%
Not at all likely

2%
Don't know

10%
Not too likely

40%
Very likely

45%
Somewhat likely

Poll taken October 2001; 502 total respondents
Source: The Gallup Organization

Number of Arab Immigrants

"Do you think the number of Arab immigrants now entering the U.S. . . .
is too many, too few, or about the right amount?"

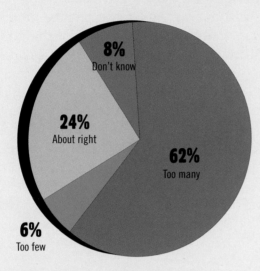

8%
Don't know

24%
About right

62%
Too many

6%
Too few

Opinions - 1993

Poll taken July 1993; 1,191 total respondents
Source: The Gallup Organization

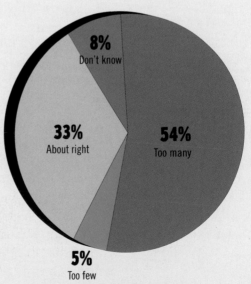

8%
Don't know

Opinions - 2002

33%
About right

54%
Too many

5%
Too few

Poll taken June 2002; 1,360 total respondents
Source: The Gallup Organization

Americans' views about immigration in general, now greatly influenced by terrorism, followed a similar pattern. The June before the attacks, a Gallup poll recorded about equal proportions of respondents who favored keeping immigration at present levels and respondents who favored a decrease (42 percent versus 41 percent). In October, one month after the attacks, a strong majority of 58 percent said they favored decreased immigration. By June 2002 less than half of all respondents, 49 percent, believed that immigration levels should be decreased. Still, as a Gallup analysis noted, although opposition to immigration was high, it never reached the levels of the mid-1990s. The same trend was evident in how people felt about Arab immigration specifically: in 2002 the proportion of Americans who thought there were too many Arab immigrants stood at 54 percent, 8 points lower than it had been in 1993.

SHOW YOUR I.D.

One issue that remained important to the public was the demand for tighter security at the borders, both along the actual physical boundaries with Mexico and Canada and at international airports. After all, at least 15 of the hijackers in the 9/11 attacks entered the United States legally, with valid visas. They managed to get approval even though nearly all had failed to complete their application forms correctly. And they were able to remain in the country even though they had violated the terms of their visas by staying past the expiration dates.

Committed to preventing such a mistake from happening again, the U.S. government sought to strengthen the security apparatus through which people are permitted to enter the country. In 2004 the Department of Homeland Security set up a system called US-Visit, which asks visa-issuing consular offices to confirm the identity of people seeking entry into the United States.

Officials do this by checking names against lists of known terrorists and using biometric technology—a sophisticated means of keeping track of individuals through eye scans and fingerprint identification. Then, upon arrival at a U.S. airport, a visitor's travel documents are supposed to be scanned, rechecked against terrorist lists, and kept in an active file to remind officials how long the person is authorized to remain in the country. "Some may argue that we're asking for too much information," said Asa Hutchinson, under secretary of border and transportation security at the Department of Homeland Security. "They may worry that it could intimidate some people and create a

A traveler is screened before boarding a flight at the Miami International Airport. The post-September 11 focus on increased security has been accompanied, some observers note, by greater scrutiny of immigrants.

chilling effect on immigration. Nothing could be further from the truth. . . . [G]ood information does not threaten immigration. Quite the contrary. The more certain we are about someone's status, the less likely we are to make a mistake that would jeopardize their status—or our safety."

The program is not without its critics. "Even today consular officers receive only a day or two of law enforcement training—hardly enough to even begin to learn the art of identifying security risks," said a *Washington Post* editorial in 2004. "Nearly three years later, it's still far too easy for a terrorist to get a visa to enter the United States." A 2005 report conducted by the Department of Homeland Security's inspector general

Immigrant Identification Cards

"Would you support or oppose a law requiring all immigrants in this country who are not legal citizens to carry a government-issued national identification card that includes information such as their fingerprints?"

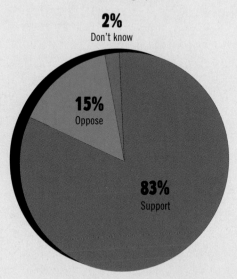

2%
Don't know

15%
Oppose

83%
Support

Poll taken June 2002; 683 total respondents
Source: The Gallup Organization

found that fewer than 3 percent of all foreign visitors who enter the country at land border crossings have their identities verified and checked against a database.

Although it would do nothing to prevent a terrorist from entering the country on a temporary "visitor" visa, one frequently proposed security measure calls for the government to issue an identity card to all immigrants. In a 2002 Gallup poll, 83 percent of respondents said they would like to see a measure requiring immigrants to carry an ID card. Identification concerns remained prevalent as Congress debated the issue in 2005.

Post-9/11 difficulties for immigrants, especially those who are Arab or Muslim, seemed unlikely to go away as reports of anti-Muslim bias incidents continued into 2005. Other immigrants also felt the impact, in part because of an American public that seemed less likely to embrace newcomers out of security concerns. But post-9/11 anxiety was not the only factor. Growing apprehension about the economic and social consequences of illegal immigration played a role too, as did general concerns about the assimilation of the largest wave of immigrants since the days of Ellis Island.

BECOMING AMERICAN?

In recent years immigration has played a significant role in American politics, not simply
because the issue is of concern to the
electorate but also because new Americans con-
stitute potentially decisive voting blocs in
national (and, in some cases, local) elections. But
immigrants and their children have proved
more than simply voters whom politicians find
it necessary to court: some have themselves
campaigned for, and won, major political office.
In 2005 Barack Obama of Illinois, the son of a
goat herder from Kenya, became the first black
man in the U.S. Senate since Edward Brooke of
Massachusetts left office in 1979. Joining Obama
in the Senate that year was Florida's Mel
Martínez, the first U.S. senator born in Cuba. In
2003 Austrian native Arnold Schwarzenegger
was elected governor of California, the nation's
most populous state, and in 2005 Los Angeles
voters made Antonio Villaraigosa the city's first
Mexican American mayor since 1872.

All of these leaders formed multi-ethnic
coalitions of voters to seal their victories, and
political analysts hailed the trend as a sign of the

(Opposite) Antonio
Villaraigosa speaks at his
inauguration ceremony,
July 1, 2005. One of a
growing number of
nationally prominent
politicians with immi-
grant connections,
Villaraigosa became the
first Mexican American
mayor of Los Angeles in
more than 130 years.

growing assimilation of the "new immigrants" — Mexicans and other Hispanics. Many found parallels between their assimilation and those of earlier immigrants over a century ago. *Newsweek* magazine compared Villaraigosa's win to the victories Irish American politicians claimed in the late 19th and early 20th centuries. In 1880 they had relied on ethnic appeal — "Shamrock politics," the magazine called it — to secure the election of William R. Grace as New York City's first Irish American mayor. Another Irish American politician, Al Smith, expanded Shamrock politics to include other allies and broaden the voter base. This strategy helped him become New York State's first Irish American governor in 1918. Smith "helped normalize the image of the Irish as mainstream Americans," *Newsweek* said. Now Villaraigosa was doing something similar for Mexican Americans.

Other analysts disagreed that immigrants were really assimilating. A few even believed that immigration was disrupting the identity of mainstream America. "In this new era, the single most immediate and most serious challenge to America's traditional identity comes from the immense and continuing immigration from Latin America," Harvard professor Samuel Huntington wrote in a controversial article for *Foreign Policy* magazine in 2004. Huntington feared that the United States was on its way to becoming a nation split into "two peoples, two cultures, and two languages."

Most of the evidence indicates that, at least when it comes to language, Huntington's alarm may be unfounded. Scholarly studies and anecdotal evidence overwhelmingly show that most of the children of immigrants not only know English, but even prefer it as their primary language.

However, the fact that someone speaks English does not necessarily mean he or she has become part of the American mainstream. Irish immigrants, for example, were once believed to be unassimilable even though they spoke English. Assimilation also is determined by how much someone has accepted attitudes and behaviors of American culture, made connections with Americans, or become familiar with the country's traditions. Will today's immigrants take these measures to become assimilated? And if so, will they melt into the proverbial pot, or will they still preserve some of their own traditions and culture?

Nobody doubts that the descendants of previous generations of immigrants—the Irish, Germans, and Scandinavians who arrived during the early and mid-19th century, as well as the eastern and southern Europeans who came later—are assimilated Americans today. However, when they first arrived in large numbers, there were serious doubts that these groups would ever blend in. Some Americans feared that the immigrants would keep to themselves in ethnic neighborhoods instead of joining the mainstream, would stay loyal to their countries of origin instead of the United States, would speak a different language instead of English, and would follow foreign customs incompatible with American life. It took a generation or more to calm those fears.

Will immigrants today follow a similar pattern and prove the present concerns to be as misguided as the nativism of the past? Or are today's immigrants truly different from those of the past, unwilling to become part of American culture? Will the multicultural values that have been advanced in recent decades encourage immigrants to stay in their private ethnic enclaves? Or can today's immigrants and their U.S.-born children manage to become assimilated Americans even as they hold on to their roots?

Such questions are important in a country with so many immigrants and people whose families have been in the country only for a generation or two. In a June 2001 Gallup survey, 7 percent of respondents identified themselves as immigrants, 12 percent as first-generation

American, and 24 percent as second-generation American. In other words, more than 4 in 10 Americans said they were immigrants, had immigrant parents, or had at least one immigrant grandparent. The 2000 census counted a foreign-born population of 28 million, including 14.5 million Latin Americans; 7.2 million Chinese, Indians, Filipinos, and other Asians; and about 4.4 million Europeans, mostly from former Soviet-bloc countries. How is American culture changing these people, and how are they changing American culture?

Part of the answer may have to do with how immigrants see themselves. What are their preferences regarding assimilating or maintaining their culture? Do they feel that they have the same economic opportunities as mainstream Americans? Another part of the answer may have to do with how society at large sees immigrants. Is it ready to accept some degree of diversity, or does it expect immigrants to sever most of their ethnic ties? Is it willing to give immigrants the full range of economic and social opportunity available to other Americans? Does it stereotype immigrants?

MIXED FEELINGS

While the proportion of Americans who think immigration was a good thing for the country in the past has remained high (it was a steady 75 percent in Gallup polls taken in 2001, 2002, and 2003), opinion on present-day immigration has frequently wavered. In a 1993 Gallup poll, 54 percent of respondents said immigration "mostly threatened" American culture. The proportion holding this view declined over the course of the 1990s, and in June 2001, a solid majority (62 percent) of respondents told Gallup that immigration was a "good thing." However, positive opinions toward immigration declined after the 9/11 attacks, only to swing back once again in 2003. That year 57 percent said immigration was good for the country, meaning that the level of support for immigration had

Do Immigrants Threaten American Culture?

"In your view, does the increasing diversity that immigrants bring to this country mostly improve
American culture or mostly threaten American culture?"

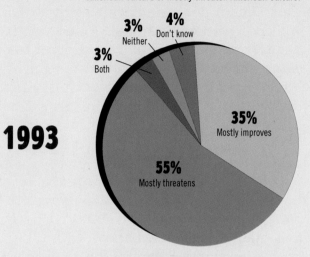

1993

3%
Both

3%
Neither

4%
Don't know

35%
Mostly improves

55%
Mostly threatens

Poll taken July 1993; 1,191 total respondents
Source: The Gallup Organization

Is Immigration a Good Thing or a Bad Thing?

"On the whole, do you think immigration is a good thing or a bad thing for this country today?"

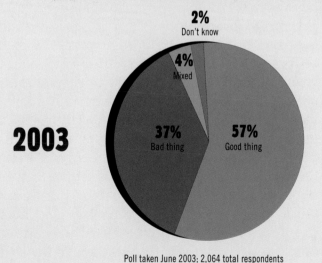

2003

2%
Don't know

4%
Mixed

37%
Bad thing

57%
Good thing

Poll taken June 2003; 2,064 total respondents
Source: The Gallup Organization

approached—but not reached—the level before the 2001 terrorist attacks.

By and large Americans seem to at least appreciate the cultural contributions of immigrants. For several years Gallup polls have shown that when it comes to "music, food and the arts" Americans believe immigrants have made valuable contributions to American culture. In 2004, for example, 44 percent of respondents thought immigrants made food, music, and the arts better, and just 10 percent thought they made it worse.

ASSIMILATION FROM DIFFERENT PERSPECTIVES

It is perhaps just as important to examine the reverse of the question as to whether immigrants are good for the United States: Is the United States good for immigrants? Some immigrants view "being American" from a different perspective than that of the native-born population. As they seek to define their role in American society, they sometimes fear some of the consequences of Americanization for their children as well as themselves.

"Many immigrant families encourage their children to pick up certain cultural competencies (such as learning English) while fiercely resisting others," write Marcelo and Carola Suárez-Orozco, a husband-and-wife team of sociologists, in their book *Children of Immigration*. "They come to see certain American attitudes and behaviors as a threat to family unity. They often view American popular culture as wanting in such realms as dating, respect of elders and peer relations. . . . In some immigrant communities, becoming 'Americanized' is synonymous with becoming sexually promiscuous."

Even immigrant children who find success worry their parents. The Suárez-Orozcos interviewed a Ghanaian taxi driver in New York City who had one son at Brown University, another at Duke, and another hoping to attend Harvard, yet he still worried about the

American friends they made and forbade them to work while still in school. "Who knows what influences they will be exposed to at a job?" the father explained. Like other immigrant parents, this man seemed certain that his children would become American, but he was worried about what kind of Americans they would become.

Another important question concerns the part Americans play in the assimilation process: How would they rate the way society treats those making a new life in the United States? How would immigrants themselves answer that question? In a 2003 Gallup poll, large segments of all the groups interviewed said immigrants were being treated well. But, as Gallup analyst Steve Crabtree noted, "there remain troubling differences in perceptions of the way the various groups are treated." The survey found that 48 percent of respondents were

A Hmong boy at his middle school in Wausau, Wisconsin. Many immigrant parents have mixed feelings about assimilation. While they want their children to succeed, they also want them to retain cherished traditions of their native culture.

either "somewhat satisfied" or "very satisfied" with society's treatment of immigrants. Ratings were higher still when respondents were asked about the treatment of two specific ethnic groups with large numbers of immigrants: 59 percent of respondents were either "somewhat satisfied" or "very satisfied" with the treatment of Hispanics, and 67 percent expressed similar satisfaction about the treatment of Asians.

However, when Gallup measured the responses of what it called "insiders"—members of the minority groups—perceptions were less upbeat. For instance, while two-thirds of non-Hispanics were satisfied with the treatment of Hispanics, only about half (51 percent) of Hispanics said they too were satisfied. Regarding the treatment of immigrants in general, 63 percent of non-Hispanic whites said they were satisfied, but just 42 percent of Hispanics and 44 percent of blacks held the same view.

BLENDING IN, STANDING OUT

Even those immigrants who are able to overlook these differences in perception and can assimilate have to consider another central question: How much of their culture should they keep and how much of American culture should they embrace as their own? Does fully embracing American culture mean that they will eventually disappear into the famous all-American melting pot?

The question assumes there was a melting pot to begin with, one that fused old immigrants together into a single, indistinct American soup. However, the metaphor is not completely accurate because in many ways the legacy of the original immigrants remains alive. "One cannot understand the character of American life today without understanding the contributions of the Irish, Italian, Jewish and other immigrant groups of a hundred years ago," Michael Barone argues in his 2001 book *The New Americans*. For Barone, this observation has obvious ramifications for how people a century from now will understand the contributions of the blacks, Latinos, and Asians of today. In the future America that he imagines, each of these groups will keep enough of its culture to have a distinctive flavor, but not so much to make "ethnic communities marked off and adversarial from each other, any more than today's America consists of unassimilated and adversarial communities of Irish, Italians and Jews."

Still, there will be problems. The Suárez-Orozcos say that even though "some immigrants are progressing up the socioeconomic ladder at a pace never before seen in the history of U.S. immigration," others "may be getting locked out of the opportunity structure—in effect creating what some have termed a 'rainbow underclass.'"

The problem, according to the Suárez-Orozcos, will not be that immigrants fail to assimilate, but that they do not assimilate into a segment of American society that offers them real opportunities. To ensure that all immigrants share the same opportunities with the American mainstream, the sociologists propose that people "cultivate and nurture the emergence of new hybrid identities" of American and immigrant peoples.

With the ongoing multicultural movement, that hybridization is, in a sense, already taking place. A century ago nobody other than immigrants encouraged newcomers to keep their culture. Today, while some Americans still insist that immigrants abandon their ethnic identity, other forces pull in the opposite direction, toward multiculturalism as the ideal model.

The American society of the future may more closely resemble a salad bowl than the melting pot of the present era. In the best scenario, there will be enough room in the bowl for every ingredient, each preserving its distinct flavor. And all ingredients will be held together by one kind of "dressing"—the unifying notion that the United States has always been a country of immigrants.

baby boomer—in the United States, a member of the generation born between the end of World War II and the mid-1960s.

bracero—the Spanish word for "migrant worker," used specifically to describe a Mexican farm worker admitted to the United States under a program that was in effect from World War II to the 1960s.

Cold War—a political and ideological struggle, lasting from the end of World War II to the late 1980s, between the U.S.-led West and the Soviet Union and its Communist allies.

illegal immigrant—a foreigner living in a country without legal authorization.

mestizo—an individual of mixed European and American Indian ancestry.

nativist—an individual who elevates the interests of native inhabitants over those of immigrants.

naturalized citizen—someone who has officially acquired the rights of nationality in a country after being born somewhere else.

permanent resident—someone who has legal permission to live in a country even though he or she is not a citizen; a legal immigrant.

pogrom—an organized massacre of Jewish people, especially in eastern Europe.

refugee—an individual permitted to enter a nation because he or she has escaped political, racial, or religious persecution.

repatriation—the act of returning a person to his or her country of origin or citizenship.

sweatshop—a factory where employees work for low pay and under unsafe conditions.

visa—a document that allows a foreigner to enter a particular country.

xenophobe—someone who hates or has an unreasonable fear of foreigners.

Antón, Alex, and Roger E. Hernández. *Cubans in America: A Vibrant History of a People in Exile.* New York: Kensington Publishing Corp., 2002.

Barone, Michael. *The New Americans: How the Melting Pot Can Work Again.* Washington, D.C.: Regnery Publishing, 2001.

Chang, Iris. *The Chinese in America: A Narrative History.* New York: Penguin Books, 2003.

Ciongoli, A. Kenneth, and Jay Parini. *Passage to Liberty: The Story of Italian Immigration and the Rebirth of America.* New York: Regan Books, 2002.

Crawford, James. *Hold Your Tongue: Bilingualism and the Politics of "English Only."* Boston: Addison-Wesley, 1992.

Daniels, Roger. *Coming to America: A History of Immigration and Ethnicity in American Life.* New York: Harper Perennial, 2002.

Miller, Kerby, and Patricia Mulholland. *Journey of Hope: The Story of Irish Immigration to America.* San Francisco: Chronicle Books, 2001.

Ramos, Jorge. *The Other Face of America.* New York: HarperCollins, 2002.

Sarna, Jonathan. *American Judaism: A History.* New Haven, Conn.: Yale University Press, 2004.

Suárez-Orozco, Carola, and Marcelo M. Suárez-Orozco. *Children of Immigration.* Cambridge, Mass.: Harvard University Press, 2001.

http://www.gallup.org

The website of the national polling institute includes polling data and analyses on hundreds of topics.

http://memory.loc.gov/learn/features/immig/alt/introduction.html

A Library of Congress website on the history of American immigration, with links to primary online resources such as documents, illustrations, and sound clips.

http://uscis.gov/graphics/index.htm

The website for U.S. Citizenship and Immigration Services has all the official information on immigrating and becoming a U.S. citizen.

http://www.census.gov/population/www/socdemo/foreign.html

The Census Bureau offers this page of links covering immigration and statistics about the foreign-born population.

http://www.cis.org

The home page of the Washington, D.C.–based Center for Immigration Studies, a group that identifies its mission as seeking "fewer immigrants but a warmer welcome for those admitted."

http://www.immigrationforum.org

The National Immigration Forum, based in Washington, D.C., is a group that promotes pro-immigration policies.

http://www.ellisislandrecords.org

This website for Ellis Island contains searchable passenger arrival records.

BOOKS

Antón, Alex, and Roger E. Hernández. *Cubans in America: A Vibrant History of a People in Exile.* New York: Kensington Publishing Corp., 2002.

Asbury, Herbert. *The Gangs of New York: An Informal History of the Underworld.* 1927. Reprint, New York: Thunder's Mouth Press, 2001. Reprint.

Barone, Michael. *The New Americans: How the Melting Pot Can Work Again.* Washington, D.C.: Regnery Publishing, 2001.

Berman, John S. *Portraits of America: Ellis Island.* New York: Barnes & Noble, 2003.

Bowles, Samuel. *Our New West: Records of Travel Between the Mississippi River and the Pacific Ocean.* Hartford, Conn.: Hartford Publishing Company, 1869.

Chang, Iris. *The Chinese in America: A Narrative History.* New York: Penguin Books, 2003.

Crawford, James. *Hold Your Tongue: Bilingualism and the Politics of "English Only."* Boston: Addison-Wesley, 1992.

Daniels, Roger. *Coming to America: A History of Immigration and Ethnicity in American Life.* New York: Harper Perennial, 2002.

Suárez-Orozco, Carola, and Marcelo M. Suárez-Orozco. *Children of Immigration.* Cambridge, Mass.: Harvard University Press, 2001.

REPORTS AND MAGAZINE AND NEWSPAPER ARTICLES

Anderson, Stuart. "The Contribution of Legal Immigration to the Social Security System." National Foundation for American Policy, February 2005.

Argetsinger, Amy. "In Arizona, 'Minutemen' Start Border Patrols: Volunteers Crusade to Stop Illegal Crossings." *Washington Post*, April 5, 2005, Page A03.

Borjas, George J. "Increasing the Supply of Labor Through Immigration: Measuring the Impact on Native-born Workers." Center for Immigration Studies, May 2004.

Camarota, Steven A. "Job Data Should Give Pause to Immigration Advocates." *Minneapolis Star Tribune*, February 20, 2005.

DePalma, Anthony. "Who Has the Work? He Who Finds the Busboys." *New York Times*, May 27, 2005.

Dinan, Stephen. "6 Million Illegals from Mexico Live in U.S." *Washington Times*, March 22, 2005.

Elliott, Andrea, and William K. Rushbaum. "Anti-Muslim Bias Seen in Charges Against Man Linked to Al Qaeda." *New York Times*, June 1, 2005.

Fulbright, Leslie. "Governor Again Lauds Minuteman Project; U.S. Lacks Will to Solve Immigration Problem, He Says." *California Chronicle*, May 9, 2005.

Levinson, Amanda. "Immigrants and Welfare Use." Migration Policy Institute, August 1, 2002.

Lovgren, Stefan. "Who Were the First Americans?" *National Geographic*, September 3, 2003.

Noonan, Kenneth. "English Immersion: A Convert Speaks Out." *Principal* 82, no. 1 (September/October 2002): 72.

Otter, Jack. "Indians Prosper in Area's High-tech Industry." *Newsday*, September 18, 2000.

Riis, Jacob A. "Feast-Days in Little Italy." *Century Magazine* 58, no. 4 (August 1899): 491.

Rodriguez, Gregory. "Why We're the New Irish: Mexican-Americans, Too, Began Apart—and Now Are a Thread in the Tapestry." *Newsweek*, May 30, 2005.

Seaborn, Mary. "Hispanics Gaining Jobs but Suffering Worse Wage Losses in U.S. Labor Force." Pew Hispanic Center, May 2, 2005.

Seper, Jerry. "Border Vigil Ends on Wary Note." *Washington Times*, May 1, 2005.

Sullivan, Kevin. "An Often-Crossed Line in the Sand: Upgraded Security at U.S. Border Hasn't Deterred Illegal Immigration from Mexico." *Washington Post*, March 7, 2005, Page A01.

CENTER FOR IMMIGRATION STUDIES
1522 K St., NW
Suite 820
Washington, DC 20005-1202
(202) 466-8185
Website: www.cis.org

CIS, a think tank devoted to research and analysis of the impact of immigration on the United States, advocates lower levels of immigration.

NATIONAL IMMIGRATION FORUM
50 F St., NW
Suite 300
Washington, DC 20001
(202) 347-0040
Website: www.immigrationforum.org

The slogan of this pro-immigration group is "To Embrace and Uphold America's Tradition as a Nation of Immigrants."

PEW HISPANIC CENTER
1615 L St., NW
Suite 700
Washington, DC 20036-5610
(202) 419-3600
Website: www.pewhispanic.org

This nonpartisan organization conducts research and public opinion surveys on various social, economic, and political topics involving Latinos in the United States.

NATIONAL COUNCIL OF LA RAZA
1126 16th St., NW
Washington, DC 20036
(202) 785-1670
Website: www.nclr.org

Founded in 1968, the NCLR is today the largest advocacy group for Hispanics in the United States.

AMERICAN IRISH HISTORICAL SOCIETY
991 Fifth Ave.
New York, NY 10028
(212) 288-2263
Website: www.aihs.org

The society, founded in 1897 to combat anti-Irish prejudice, defines its mission as "to place permanently on record the story of the Irish in America from the earliest settlement to the present day, justly, impartially, [and] fully. . . ."

ARAB AMERICAN INSTITUTE
1600 K St., NW
Suite 601
Washington, DC 20006
(202) 429-9210
Website: www.aaiusa.org

This nonprofit organization, founded in 1985, seeks to mobilize Americans of Arab descent for greater civic participation and political empowerment.

NATIONAL ITALIAN AMERICAN FOUNDATION
1860 19th St., NW
Washington, DC 20009
(202) 387-0600
Website: www.niaf.org

The NIAF seeks to preserve and protect Italian American heritage and culture.

Numbers in **bold italics** refer to captions.

Page:
3:      Library of Congress
8:      Library of Congress
10:     PhotoDisc
14:     © OTTN Publishing
18:     Library of Congress
22:     Library of Congress
25:     Library of Congress
26:     Library of Congress
28:     Library of Congress
29:     Library of Congress
31:     Keystone/Getty Images
34:     Library of Congress
37:     Library of Congress
38:     © OTTN Publishing
40:     Library of Congress
42:     © OTTN Publishing
45:     © OTTN Publishing
47:     Tim Chapman/Miami Herald/Getty Images
48:     © OTTN Publishing
50:     Pool/AFP/Getty Images
52:     Barbara Laing/Time Life Pictures/Getty Images
55:     © OTTN Publishing
59:     © OTTN Publishing
62:     Tim Boyle/Getty Images
64:     Spencer Platt/Getty Images
69:     Dirck Halstead/Time Life Pictures/Getty Images
72:     Scott Olson/Getty Images
75:     © OTTN Publishing
77:     © OTTN Publishing
79:     © OTTN Publishing
81:     David McNew/Getty Images
83:     Mark Wilson/Getty Images
86:     David McNew/Getty Images
88:     © OTTN Publishing
91:     © OTTN Publishing
92:     © OTTN Publishing
93:     © OTTN Publishing
95:     Joe Raedle/Getty Images
96:     © OTTN Publishing
98:     David McNew/Getty Images
103:    © OTTN Publishing
105:    Steve Liss/Time Life Pictures/Getty Images

For almost three-quarters of a century, the GALLUP POLL has measured the attitudes and opinions of the American public about the major events and the most important political, social, and economic issues of the day. Founded in 1935 by Dr. George Gallup, the Gallup Poll was the world's first public opinion poll based on scientific sampling procedures. For most of its history, the Gallup Poll was sponsored by the nation's largest newspapers, which published two to four of Gallup's public opinion reports each week. Poll findings, which covered virtually every major news event and important issue facing the nation and the world, were reported in a variety of media. More recently, the poll has been conducted in partnership with CNN and USA Today. All of Gallup's findings, including many opinion trends dating back to the 1930s and 1940s, are accessible at www.gallup.com.

ALEC M. GALLUP is chairman of The Gallup Poll in the United States, and Chairman of The Gallup Organization Ltd. in Great Britain. He also serves as a director of The Gallup Organisation, Europe; Gallup China; and Gallup Hungary. He has been employed by Gallup since 1959 and has directed or played key roles in many of the company's most ambitious and innovative projects, including Gallup's 2002 "Survey of Nine Islamic Nations"; the "Global Cities Project"; the "Global Survey on Attitudes Towards AIDS"; the 25-nation "Health of The Planet Survey"; and the ongoing "Survey of Consumer Attitudes and Lifestyles in China." Mr. Gallup also oversees several annual "social audits," including "Black and White Relations in the United States," an investigation of attitudes and perceptions concerning the state of race relations, and "Survey of the Public's Attitudes Toward the Public Schools," which tracks attitudes on educational issues.

Mr. Gallup's educational background includes undergraduate work at Princeton University and the University of Iowa. He undertook graduate work in communications and journalism at Stanford University, and studied marketing and advertising research at New York University. His publications include *The Great American Success Story* (with George Gallup, Jr.; Dow Jones-Irwin, 1986), *Presidential Approval: A Source Book* (with George Edwards; Johns Hopkins University Press, 1990), *The Gallup Poll Cumulative Index: Public Opinion* 1935–1997 (Scholarly Resources, 1999), and *British Political Opinion 1937–2000: The Gallup Polls* (with Anthony King and Robert Wybrow; Politicos Publishing, 2001).

ROGER E. HERNANDEZ is the most widely read nationally syndicated columnist writing on Hispanic American issues and is coauthor of *Cubans in America*, an illustrated history of the Cuban presence in the United States. He also teaches journalism and English composition at Rutgers University and the New Jersey Institute of Technology, where he is Writer-in-Residence.